# WeightWatchers®

### Spice and flavour for every occasion

# Simply Spicy

D0766884

First published in Great Britain by Simon & Schuster UK Ltd, 2013
A CBS Company

www.simonandschuster.co.uk

Simon & Schuster Australia, Sydney
Simon & Schuster India, New Delhi

**Weight Watchers Publications:** Jane Griffiths, Linda Palmer and Nina McKerlie.

**Recipes written by:** Sue Ashworth, Sue Beveridge, Tamsin Burnett-Hall,
Cas Clarke, Siân Davies, Roz Denny, Nicola Graimes, Becky Johnson,
Kim Morphew, Joy Skipper, Penny Stephens and Wendy Veale as well
as Weight Watchers Leaders and Members.

**Photography by:** Iain Bagwell, Steve Baxter, Steve Lee, Juliet Piddington
and William Shaw.
**Project editor:** Nicki Lampon.
**Design and typesetting:** Martin Lampon.

Colour reproduction by Dot Gradations Ltd, UK.
Printed and bound in China.

A CIP catalogue for this book is available from the British Library

ISBN 978-1-47111-087-0

1 2 3 4 5 6 7 8 9 10

Pictured on the title page: Butterflied tandoori chicken p92.
Pictured on the Introduction: Tandoori paneer and vegetable biryani p134, Thai
salmon surprise p82, Chicken tikka masala p84.

# WeightWatchers®

## Spice and flavour for every occasion

# Simply Spicy

SIMON &
SCHUSTER
ILLUSTRATED

London · New York · Sydney · Toronto · New Delhi

A CBS COMPANY

Weight Watchers **ProPoints** Weight Loss System is a simple way to lose weight. As part of the Weight Watchers **ProPoints** plan you'll enjoy eating delicious, healthy, filling foods that help to keep you feeling satisfied for longer and in control of your portions.

 This symbol denotes a vegetarian recipe and assumes that, where relevant, free range eggs, vegetarian cheese, vegetarian virtually fat free fromage frais, vegetarian low fat crème fraîche and vegetarian low fat yogurts are used. Virtually fat free fromage frais, low fat crème fraîche and low fat yogurts may contain traces of gelatine so they are not always vegetarian. Please check the labels.

 This symbol denotes a dish that can be frozen. Unless otherwise stated, you can freeze the finished dish for up to 3 months. Defrost thoroughly and reheat until the dish is piping hot throughout.

## Recipe notes

**Egg size:** Medium sized, unless otherwise stated.

**Raw eggs:** Only the freshest eggs should be used. Pregnant women, the elderly and children should avoid recipes with eggs that are not fully cooked or raw.

**All fruits and vegetables:** Medium sized, unless otherwise stated.

**Stock:** Stock cubes are used in recipes, unless otherwise stated. These should be prepared according to packet instructions.

**Recipe timings:** These are approximate and meant to be guidelines. Please note that the preparation time includes all the steps up to and following the main cooking time(s).

**Microwaves:** Timings and temperatures are for a standard 800 W microwave. If necessary, adjust your own microwave.

**Low fat spread:** Where a recipe states to use a low fat spread, a light spread with a fat content of no less than 38% should be used.

**Low fat soft cheese:** Where low fat soft cheese is specified in a recipe, this refers to soft cheese with a fat content of less than 5%.

# Contents

# Introduction

There's nothing like a little spice to add interest to your food, so jazz up your meals with *Simply Spicy* – packed full of fantastic recipes from the best of Weight Watchers cookbooks.

Spicy food does not just mean curries, and there are so many different ways to add a little bit of spice to your food. Liven up your lunch with a little chilli, brighten a plain piece of meat or fish with a spicy side dish, or treat the family to a home-made spicy supper instead of a take-away. From a Cajun Steak Muffin for one to Chermoula Curried Pork for six, there are recipes here for all occasions. So give them a go, and once you feel confident you'll be ready to start experimenting with other dishes, adding spice to your life.

## About Weight Watchers

For more than 40 years Weight Watchers has been helping people around the world to lose weight using a long term sustainable approach. Weight Watchers successful weight loss system is based on four tried and trusted principles:

- Eating healthily
- Being more active
- Adjusting behaviour to help weight loss
- Getting support in weekly meetings

Our unique ***ProPoints*** system empowers you to manage your food plan and make wise recipe choices for a healthier, happier you.

To find out more about Weight Watchers and the ***ProPoints*** values for these recipes contact Customer Service on 0845 345 1500.

## Buying spices

It is always worth keeping a few spices in your store cupboard and it is always worth investing in some quality ingredients. This way you'll always have ingredients to create a tasty meal.

- Ground spices – check the dates on any dried spices in your cupboard and buy fresh ones if you need to. If you live near an ethnic grocer or supermarket, try buying from there instead of your regular supermarket. Prices can sometimes be lower and there will be a great choice. If possible, buy little and often so that the spices are as fresh as possible, and keep them in a cool dark place. Remember to replace them regularly if you don't use them up.
- Whole spices – if you want to grind your own spices you will need to invest in a mortar and pestle or a spice grinder, if you don't have one already. The colour and aroma of ready-ground spices can fade quickly, and freshly ground ones have far more flavour.
- Curry and spice pastes – these are available in the ethnic foods departments of large supermarkets and from specialist retailers. Don't be afraid to use them and try a few to find the ones you like best.
- Ready-prepared lemongrass, ginger and garlic – these are great as an emergency standby, so don't be afraid to use them when necessary.

Toasting whole spices releases their aroma. If you are going to grind your own, you may want to toast them first by dry-frying them in a pan for a minute or two until they give off a warm aroma. Be careful not to let them burn.

## Storing and freezing

Once you have mastered the art of cooking delicious, healthy meals, you may want to make extra and store or freeze it for a later date.

- Store any leftovers in sealed containers in the fridge and use them up within a day or two.
- Wrap any food to be frozen in rigid containers or strong freezer bags. This is important to stop foods contaminating each other or getting freezer burn.
- Label the containers or bags with the contents and date – your freezer should have a star marking that tells you how long you can keep different types of frozen food.
- Never freeze warm food – always let it cool completely first.
- Never freeze food that has already been frozen and defrosted.
- Freeze food in portions, then you can take out as little or as much as you need each time.
- Defrost what you need in the fridge, making sure you put anything that might have juices on a covered plate or in a container.

## Shopping hints and tips

When you're going around the supermarket it's tempting to pick up foods you like and put them in your trolley without thinking about how you will use them. So, a good plan is to decide what you want to cook before you go shopping and make a list of what you need.

We've added a checklist here for some of the store cupboard ingredients used in this book. Just add fresh ingredients in your regular shop and you'll be ready to cook the wonderful recipes in *Simply Spicy*.

# Store cupboard checklist

- [ ] apricots, canned in natural juice
- [ ] bamboo shoots, canned
- [ ] barbecue sauce
- [ ] beans, canned (various types)
- [ ] Cajun spice mix
- [ ] cardamom pods
- [ ] cayenne pepper
- [ ] chick peas, canned
- [ ] chilli (powder and flakes)
- [ ] chilli sauce, sweet
- [ ] cinnamon (ground and sticks)
- [ ] coconut milk, reduced fat
- [ ] cooking spray, calorie controlled
- [ ] coriander (seeds and ground)
- [ ] cornflour
- [ ] couscous, dried

- [ ] crab meat, canned
- [ ] cumin (seeds and ground)
- [ ] curry (powder and pastes)
- [ ] fennel seeds
- [ ] fish sauce
- [ ] flour (plain white and wholemeal)
- [ ] garam masala
- [ ] ginger, ground
- [ ] honey, clear
- [ ] horseradish sauce
- [ ] jalapeño peppers, in a jar
- [ ] jerk seasoning
- [ ] lentils, dried red
- [ ] mustard (English, Dijon and wholegrain)
- [ ] mustard seeds
- [ ] noodles, dried
- [ ] oil, olive
- [ ] passata
- [ ] pasta, dried

- [ ] peppercorns
- [ ] pepperdew peppers, in a jar
- [ ] polenta, dried
- [ ] ras el hanout
- [ ] rice, dried (basmati)
- [ ] saffron
- [ ] salt
- [ ] soy sauce
- [ ] star anise
- [ ] stock cubes
- [ ] sugar, caster
- [ ] Tabasco sauce
- [ ] Thai 7 spice
- [ ] tomato ketchup
- [ ] tomato purée
- [ ] tomatoes, canned
- [ ] turmeric
- [ ] vinegar (balsamic and white wine)
- [ ] Worcestershire sauce

# Lunches, starters and sides

# Spicy beef and noodle soup

Serves 2
**311 calories** per serving
Takes 30 minutes

**calorie controlled cooking
  spray**
**300 g (10½ oz) lean rump beef,
  cut into thin strips**
**1 litre (1¾ pints) beef stock**
**2 lemongrass stalks, tough
  outer leaves removed,
  chopped**
**2 red chillies, de-seeded and
  diced**
**juice of 2 limes**
**125 g (4½ oz) dried thread egg
  noodles**
**75 g (2¾ oz) mange tout**
**110 g (4 oz) baby corn**
**a few fresh coriander leaves,
  to garnish**

*A tangy and slightly hot soup with strips of beef and
noodles.*

**1** Lightly spray a large, lidded, non stick pan with the
cooking spray and heat until hot. Add the beef and stir-fry for
3–5 minutes until browned all over.

**2** Add the stock, lemongrass, chillies and lime juice. Bring
to the boil, cover and simmer for 10 minutes until the beef is
tender.

**3** Add the noodles, mange tout and baby corn. Bring to the
boil. Simmer gently for 5 minutes until the noodles are cooked
and the vegetables tender. Garnish with the coriander before
serving.

**Variation...** Try this recipe with the equivalent weight of
sliced skinless boneless chicken breast instead of the beef.

# Spicy chicken laksa

Serves 4
**394 calories** per serving
Takes 30 minutes to prepare,
  20 minutes to cook

**calorie controlled cooking
  spray**
**4 x 150 g (5½ oz) skinless
  boneless chicken breasts,
  cut into bite size pieces**
**1 onion, sliced finely**
**1 red pepper, de-seeded and
  sliced finely**
**2 tablespoons tom yum paste**
**450 ml (16 fl oz) chicken stock**
**400 ml can reduced fat
  coconut milk**
**125 g (4½ oz) sugar snap peas**
**100 g (3½ oz) dried
  wholewheat noodles**
**220 g can bamboo shoots in
  water, drained**
**½ x 25 g packet fresh
  coriander, leaves only**
**lime wedges, to serve**

*Tom yum is a Thai spiced paste used for making traditional
hot and sour soups and is available from most large
supermarkets. If you can't find it, use 2 tablespoons of
red Thai curry paste instead.*

**1** Heat a deep, lidded, non stick saucepan and spray with
the cooking spray. Add the chicken pieces and cook for
5 minutes, stirring until brown. You may need to do this in
batches. Remove and set aside.

**2** Add the onion and pepper to the saucepan and cook for
3–4 minutes until softened but not coloured. Stir in the tom
yum paste and cook for 1 minute. Return the chicken pieces
to the pan and pour in the stock and coconut milk. Bring to the
boil, cover and simmer for 20 minutes.

**3** Add the sugar snap peas, noodles and bamboo shoots. Cook,
uncovered, for 2–3 minutes until tender, stirring occasionally to
break up the noodles. Serve immediately in bowls, topped with
the coriander and with lime wedges on the side.

🅥 **Variation...** For a vegetarian version, replace the chicken
with a 350 g packet of Quorn Chicken Style Pieces and use
vegetable stock instead of chicken.

# Sweet and spicy tomato soup

Serves 6

**65 calories** per serving

Takes 10 minutes to prepare,
35 minutes to cook

**750 g (1 lb 10 oz) large vine
tomatoes, halved**

**2 red peppers, de-seeded and
quartered**

**1 yellow pepper, de-seeded
and quartered**

**3 red chillies**

**2 fresh rosemary sprigs**

**calorie controlled cooking
spray**

**1.2 litres (2 pints) hot
vegetable stock**

**freshly ground black pepper**

To serve

**6 tablespoons virtually fat free
plain fromage frais**

**3 tablespoons snipped fresh
chives**

*This soup makes a great meal in a mug for Bonfire night.*

**1** Preheat the oven to Gas Mark 6/200°C/fan oven 180°C.
Place the tomatoes, peppers, whole chillies and rosemary in a
large roasting tin. Spray with the cooking spray and roast for
35 minutes until beginning to char.

**2** Transfer the contents of the roasting tin to a food processor
or use a hand blender, add a little of the stock and blend until
smooth. Sieve to remove any pips, pushing as much pulp
through as possible, and season with black pepper.

**3** Return the soup to the pan with the remaining stock and
warm gently until hot. Serve each bowl with a dollop of
fromage frais and some chives sprinkled on top.

**Tip...** Although vine tomatoes are more expensive, they do
retain more flavour and so enhance the soup.

# Thai beef salad

**Serves 2**
**161 calories** per serving
Takes 10 minutes

4 x 30 g (1¼ oz) slices lean roast beef, shredded
1 teaspoon grated fresh root ginger
½ teaspoon Thai 7 spice
1½ tablespoons mature balsamic vinegar
2 spring onions, sliced finely
75 g (2¾ oz) radishes, sliced finely
¼ cucumber, diced
2 large tomatoes, chopped
150 g (5½ oz) beansprouts

*A brilliant way to use up the Sunday roast. Serve with two wholewheat crispbreads per person.*

**1** Mix together the beef, ginger, Thai 7 spice and balsamic vinegar in a large bowl.

**2** Add the spring onions, radishes, cucumber, tomatoes and beansprouts. Gently toss to mix. Divide between two plates and serve.

# Chilli crab and mango salad

Serves 4
**205 calories** per serving
Takes 5 minutes

**240 g (8½ oz) fresh crab meat
or 2 x 120 g cans white crab
meat, drained**
**1 cucumber, grated**
**8 small pink radishes, halved
and sliced thinly**
**2 ripe mangos or papayas,
peeled, stoned or de-seeded
and sliced**
**2 teaspoons caster sugar**
**1½ teaspoons fish sauce or
soy sauce**
**1 teaspoon dried chilli flakes**
**juice of 2 limes**
**salt**

To garnish
**1 small red chilli, de-seeded
and chopped**
**50 g (1¾ oz) roasted peanuts,
chopped**
**a small bunch of fresh chives
or coriander, chopped**

*This recipe is based on a South East Asian salad and is
delicious.*

**1** Put all the ingredients except the garnish in a bowl and toss
together gently.

**2** Pile on to serving plates, sprinkle with the chilli, peanuts and
chives or coriander and serve.

# Warm spicy sausage and spinach salad

Serves 2
**292 calories** per serving
Takes 25–30 minutes

**4 thick reduced fat pork
sausages**
**150 g (5½ oz) cherry tomatoes**
**225 g (8 oz) baby spinach,
washed**
**salt and freshly ground black
pepper**

For the dressing
**1 tablespoon balsamic vinegar**
**1 small red chilli, de-seeded
and chopped finely or
¼ teaspoon dried chilli
flakes**
**1 small garlic clove, crushed**
**2 teaspoons olive oil**

*Salads aren't just for summer. This one hits the spot all
year round.*

**1** Preheat the oven to Gas Mark 7/220°C/fan oven 200°C.
Place the sausages and tomatoes in a roasting tin. Season
and cook for 15–20 minutes, shaking the tin occasionally,
until the sausages are browned and the tomatoes softened.
Once the sausages are cooked, slice them diagonally into bite
size pieces.

**2** Mix together the dressing ingredients in a bowl and add the
spinach. Season and toss together.

**3** Divide the spinach between two serving plates. Spoon the
hot tomatoes and sausage slices on top and serve.

# Eastern vegetable wrap

Serves 1
**256 calories** per serving
Takes 10 minutes

**½ red pepper, de-seeded and sliced**
**½ small courgette, sliced**
**2 teaspoons sweet chilli sauce**
**1 soft flour tortilla**
**1 tablespoon reduced fat houmous**
**25 g (1 oz) baby spinach, washed**
**25 g (1 oz) mild pepperdew peppers from a jar, drained and sliced**
**salt and freshly ground black pepper**

*This is a tasty vegetarian version of the recipe on page 38.*

**1** Preheat the grill to medium high. Place the pepper and courgette slices on the grill pan and grill for 3–5 minutes, turning halfway through, until lightly charred.

**2** In a bowl, mix the grilled vegetables with the chilli sauce until coated. Put the flour tortilla on a clean board and spread the houmous all over it. Season and top with the baby spinach.

**3** Scatter over the chilli vegetables and top with the sliced pepperdew peppers. Roll up the tortilla, folding in the ends. Cut the tortilla in half and wrap in cling film until needed.

# Vegetable samosas

Serves 4

**145 calories** per serving

Takes 25 minutes to prepare,
15 minutes to cook

250 g (9 oz) potatoes, peeled
and diced

200 g (7 oz) carrots, peeled
and diced

50 g (1¾ oz) frozen peas

calorie controlled cooking
spray

1 teaspoon medium curry
powder

½ teaspoon black mustard
seeds

a pinch of hot chilli powder

2 tablespoons chopped fresh
coriander

4 x 45 g (1½ oz) sheets
filo pastry, measuring
50 x 24 cm (20 x 9½ inches)

salt and freshly ground black
pepper

*These spicy vegetable filled samosas are perfect for a lunchbox.*

**1** Preheat the oven to Gas Mark 5/190°C/fan oven 170°C.

**2** Bring a pan of water to the boil, add the potatoes and carrots and cook for 7–8 minutes until tender. Drain. Tip the frozen peas into a sieve and run under the cold tap to defrost.

**3** Spray a non stick saucepan with the cooking spray, add the spices and peas and stir fry for 1 minute. Add the potatoes and carrots and mix together well, lightly crushing some of the vegetables.

**4** Remove the pan from the heat and stir in the coriander and plenty of seasoning. Tip out on to a plate to cool slightly and divide into eight portions.

**5** Cut each sheet of filo pastry in half widthways. Stack the pieces together and keep them covered with a damp towel while you work.

**6** Take a piece of filo and spray with the cooking spray. Fold in half lengthways to give a long narrow strip. Place a spoonful of the spicy vegetables near the top, bring one corner of the pastry down over the filling and then fold the pastry up in a series of triangle shapes. Place the samosa on a non stick baking tray with the end of the pastry tucked underneath. Repeat with the remaining filo pastry and vegetables.

**7** Spray the samosas with the cooking spray and bake in the oven for 15 minutes until golden brown and crisp. Let them cool slightly before eating.

# Cajun steak muffin

Serves 1
**247 calories**
Takes 6 minutes

**¼–½ teaspoon Cajun spice mix**

**60 g (2 oz) sandwich steak or minute steak, trimmed of visible fat**

**calorie controlled cooking spray**

**1 white or wholemeal English muffin, split**

**1 tablespoon 0% fat Greek yogurt**

**1 tomato, sliced**

**1 leaf from a round lettuce or shredded Iceberg lettuce**

*A great treat for a speedy lunch, especially at the weekend.*

**1** Sprinkle the Cajun spice mix (use ¼ or ½ teaspoon, depending on desired degree of spiciness) over both sides of the steak.

**2** Preheat a non stick frying pan and lightly spray with the cooking spray. Fry the steak for 1–1½ minutes on each side, to your liking.

**3** Meanwhile, lightly toast the muffin and spread the yogurt on to the cut sides. Top with the sliced tomato, lettuce and steak, and eat straightaway.

**Ⓥ Variation...** For a vegetarian version, replace the steak with a large flat mushroom, sliced and fried as above.

# Tex Mex tortilla

Serves 2
**232 calories** per serving
Takes 20 minutes

**calorie controlled cooking spray**
**1 small onion, chopped roughly**
**1 red pepper, chopped roughly**
**1 green pepper, chopped roughly**
**2 garlic cloves, crushed**
**a pinch of dried chilli flakes**
**½ teaspoon ground cumin**
**4 eggs**
**2 heaped tablespoons chopped fresh coriander**
**salt and freshly ground black pepper**

*Bursting with flavour, this mouth-watering tortilla can be served warm from the pan, or left to cool and cut into wedges for a packed lunch.*

**1** Lightly spray a lidded non stick frying pan with the cooking spray. Fry the onion and peppers for 5 minutes until browned and then stir in the garlic, chilli flakes and cumin. Cover the pan and cook for 2 minutes.

**2** Preheat the grill to medium.

**3** Beat the eggs with some seasoning and stir in the coriander. Pour over the vegetables and reduce the heat to low. Cook for 5 minutes until the bottom of the tortilla is set.

**4** Place the pan under the grill for 2 minutes to finish off the top and then serve, cut into wedges.

# Red hot legs

Serves 4
**170 calories** per serving
Takes 25 minutes
❄

8 chicken drumsticks, skinned
1 teaspoon garlic purée
4 tablespoons tomato ketchup
1 tablespoon clear honey
1 tablespoon Dijon mustard
1 teaspoon chilli paste or
   ½ teaspoon chilli powder
a dash of Worcestershire
   sauce
salt

To serve
onion rings
lemon wedges

*Serve these drumsticks with celery sticks, tomato wedges and crisp green pepper chunks. If you have the time, make some coleslaw; otherwise buy a 95% fat free ready-prepared one.*

**1** Place the drumsticks in a shallow flameproof dish. Mix together the garlic purée, tomato ketchup, honey, mustard, chilli paste or powder and Worcestershire sauce and season with salt. Pour the sauce over the drumsticks, coating them thoroughly.

**2** Preheat the grill to medium. Cook the drumsticks for 15–20 minutes, turning frequently, until tender.

**3** Serve hot, with the lemon wedges and fresh onion rings.

**Tip...** The recipe suggests raw onion rings but if you don't like raw onion, pop them under the grill for a few moments while the drumsticks are cooking.

# Mini meatballs with spicy dipping sauce

Serves 4
**89 calories** per serving
Takes 45 minutes
❄ (meatballs only)

**For the meatballs**
**200 g (7 oz) lean minced beef**
**2 tablespoons snipped fresh chives**
**2 tablespoons finely chopped fresh parsley**
**1 egg white**
**calorie controlled cooking spray**
**salt and freshly ground black pepper**

**For the dipping sauce**
**227 g can chopped tomatoes with garlic**
**2 tablespoons tomato purée**
**1 teaspoon chilli powder**

*These make great party nibbles, or you can serve them as a starter to share for an informal dinner.*

**1** In a bowl, mix together the mince, chives, parsley and egg white until well combined. Season. Using wet hands, shape into 12 equal sized balls.

**2** Lightly spray a non stick frying pan with the cooking spray and heat until hot. Add the meatballs and cook, turning occasionally, for 8–10 minutes until browned and cooked through (you may need to do this in batches – keep all the meatballs warm as you do so).

**3** Combine the sauce ingredients and heat in a small pan for 2–3 minutes until hot.

**4** Serve the meatballs with cocktail sticks for dipping the meatballs into the sauce.

**Tip...** For a main course for two, serve the hot meatballs and sauce on top of 60 g (2 oz) dried pasta per person, cooked according to the packet instructions.

# Thai fish cakes

Serves 4
**155 calories** per serving
Takes 20 minutes
❄

350 g (12 oz) skinless cod
  fillet, cut into bite size
  pieces
1 garlic clove, crushed
1 tablespoon Thai green curry
  paste
2 tablespoons fish sauce
2 tablespoons chopped fresh
  coriander
1 tablespoon cornflour
1 egg
75 g (2¾ oz) fine green beans
1 tablespoon sunflower oil

*These spicy fish cakes are delicious served with a chilli sauce for dipping.*

**1** Place the cod in a food processor with the garlic, curry paste, fish sauce, coriander, cornflour and egg. Blend until thoroughly combined.

**2** Finely slice the green beans into thin discs and fold into the fish mixture. Using wet hands, shape the mixture into 12 small cakes.

**3** Heat the oil in a large non stick frying pan and fry the cakes for 10 minutes, turning halfway through cooking. Drain on kitchen towel and serve hot.

**Variation...** A little canned white crab meat can be used in place of some of the cod. Use 225 g (8 oz) cod and 125 g (4½ oz) canned drained white crab meat.

# Chicken tikka lunchbox

Serves 1

**318 calories**

Takes 35 minutes +
30 minutes marinating

**For the chicken tikka**

**3 tablespoons low fat natural
yogurt**

**1 teaspoon medium curry
powder**

**1 teaspoon tomato purée**

**100 g (3½ oz) skinless
boneless chicken breast**

**For the salad**

**40 g (1½ oz) dried basmati
rice**

**1 teaspoon chopped fresh
mint or a pinch of dried mint**

**5 cm (2 inches) cucumber,
diced**

**½ yellow pepper, de-seeded
and diced**

**salt and freshly ground black
pepper**

*A satisfying portable lunch that makes a great change
from everyday sandwiches.*

**1** Mix together the yogurt, curry powder and tomato purée.
Add the chicken breast, turn to coat and place in the fridge to
marinate for 30 minutes.

**2** Meanwhile, bring a pan of water to the boil, add the
rice and cook for 10 minutes, or according to the packet
instructions. Rinse in cold water and drain well. Preheat
the grill to medium high.

**3** Cook the chicken under the grill for 10–12 minutes or until
cooked through, turning halfway through the cooking time.
Leave to cool and then slice.

**4** Tip the rice into a bowl with the mint, cucumber and
pepper and mix together. Season to taste and then transfer to
a lunchbox and top with the chicken tikka slices. Store in the
fridge until ready to eat – it will keep for up to 2 days.

# Eastern lamb wrap

Serves 1
**313 calories**
Takes 5 minutes

40 g (1½ oz) cooked lean
  lamb, shredded
2 teaspoons sweet chilli sauce
1 soft flour tortilla
1 tablespoon reduced fat
  houmous
25 g (1 oz) baby spinach,
  washed
25 g (1 oz) mild pepperdew
  peppers from a jar, drained
  and sliced
salt and freshly ground black
  pepper

*Leftover Sunday roast makes an ideal lunchbox filler.*

**1** In a bowl, mix the lamb with the chilli sauce until coated. Put the flour tortilla on a clean board and spread the houmous all over it. Season and top with the baby spinach.

**2** Scatter over the chilli lamb and top with the sliced pepperdew peppers. Roll up the tortilla, folding in the ends. Cut the tortilla in half and wrap in cling film until needed.

**Variation...** For a wonderful vegetarian version, see the recipe on page 26.

# Prawns in 'red-hot' cocktail sauce

Serves 4
**75 calories** per serving
Takes 5 minutes

2 tablespoons white wine
  vinegar
2 tablespoons soy sauce
6 tablespoons tomato ketchup
½ teaspoon Tabasco sauce or
  hot pepper sauce
1 small onion, grated
200 g (7 oz) cooked peeled
  prawns, defrosted if frozen
lettuce leaves, to serve

*Served with lettuce, this makes a perfect starter. With toast
or slices of wholemeal bread it makes a very tasty lunch
dish.*

**1** Mix together the vinegar, soy sauce, tomato ketchup and
Tabasco sauce or hot pepper sauce. Add the onion and prawns
and mix well.

**2** Place the lettuce leaves in serving glasses or on small plates
and top with the prawn mixture.

**Variation...** Substitute the prawns with 200 g (7 oz) cooked
mixed seafood, defrosted if frozen.

# Saag paneer

Serves 2
**155 calories** per serving
Takes 30 minutes

**225 g (8 oz) spinach, washed and chopped roughly**

**a kettleful of boiling water**

**calorie controlled cooking spray**

**110 g (4 oz) paneer, cubed**

**1 red chilli, de-seeded and chopped (optional)**

**2 garlic cloves, chopped**

**2 cm (¾ inch) fresh root ginger, grated**

**2 teaspoons garam masala**

**2 tablespoons whipping cream**

**salt and freshly ground black pepper**

**fresh coriander leaves, to serve**

*Paneer is an Indian cheese available from larger supermarkets or specialist stores. Serve this dish as an accompaniment or on its own.*

**1** Place the spinach in a large colander and pour over boiling water until it has just wilted. Set aside to drain.

**2** Lightly spray a non stick frying pan with the cooking spray and heat until hot. Add the paneer and fry for 3–4 minutes until the cubes are golden. Add the chilli, if using, garlic, ginger and garam masala. Stir-fry for 1–2 minutes.

**3** Remove the pan from the heat. Stir in the spinach and 4 tablespoons of water. Return to the heat, simmer for 10 minutes and then stir in the cream. Season and garnish with the coriander leaves before serving.

# Spicy potatoes

Serves 4

**165 calories** per serving

Takes 8 minutes to prepare,
25–30 minutes to cook

½ teaspoon mustard seeds

½ teaspoon cumin seeds

**600 g (1 lb 5 oz) potatoes,
peeled and chopped**

½ teaspoon cayenne pepper

½ teaspoon turmeric

½ teaspoon grated fresh root
ginger

2 tablespoons ground
coriander

4 tomatoes, chopped

1 tablespoon desiccated
coconut

salt

*A delicious way of serving potatoes, with fresh tomatoes
and lots of spice.*

**1** Place the mustard seeds and cumin seeds in a lidded non
stick pan over a medium heat. When they start to 'pop', add the
potatoes, cayenne pepper, turmeric, ginger and coriander. Mix
really well to coat the potatoes in the spices.

**2** Add 100 ml (3½ fl oz) of water, stir gently and bring to a
simmer. Cover and simmer for 15 minutes.

**3** Add the tomatoes and coconut, season with salt and stir
well. Cover again and cook for another 10–15 minutes until the
potatoes are tender. Serve.

# Seven spice beans

**Serves 2**
**117 calories** per serving
Takes 10 minutes

150 g (5½ oz) frozen soya
  beans
½ a kettleful of boiling water
calorie controlled cooking
  spray
1 garlic clove, sliced
1 Thai red chilli, de-seeded
  and sliced finely (optional)
2 spring onions, sliced finely
½ teaspoon Thai 7 spice
a few drops of fish sauce
juice of ½ a lime

*Thai red chillies are very hot, so it's best to use large red chillies if you want less of a kick.*

**1** Put the soya beans in a pan and cover with the boiling water. Bring to the boil and simmer for 3 minutes. Drain and refresh in cold water. Drain again.

**2** Heat a wok or non stick frying pan until hot and spray with the cooking spray. Stir-fry the garlic, chilli, if using, and spring onions for 1 minute.

**3** Add the Thai 7 spice and soya beans and stir-fry for 1 minute. Season with the fish sauce and lime juice. Serve immediately.

# Around the world

# Keralan lamb kebabs

Serves 2
**256 calories** per serving
Takes 20 minutes
❄ (kebabs only)

**200 g (7 oz) lean minced lamb**
**1½ teaspoons garam masala**
**5 freeze dried curry leaves, crushed**
**1 spring onion, chopped finely**
**1 preserved lemon, pips removed, chopped finely**
**½ x 410 g can apricot halves in natural juice, drained**
**3 tablespoons virtually fat free plain fromage frais**
**a generous pinch of cayenne pepper**
**¼ teaspoon black onion seeds**
**salt and freshly ground black pepper**

*Indian-style kofta kebabs with a fruity dipping sauce make a great simple supper. Serve with a generous mixed salad.*

**1** Preheat the grill to medium high. In a bowl, mix together the mince, garam masala, curry leaves, spring onion and preserved lemon. Divide the mixture into quarters and shape each around a metal or wooden skewer like a sausage. Put on a grill tray and cook for 10 minutes, turning until cooked through.

**2** Meanwhile, in a food processor or using a hand blender, whizz together the apricot halves, fromage frais and cayenne pepper. Stir in the onion seeds and check the seasoning. Serve the kebabs with the apricot dipping sauce.

**Tip...** If using wooden skewers, soak them in water for 30 minutes beforehand to prevent them from burning.

# Californian salsa salmon

Serves 4

**415 calories** per serving

Takes 10 minutes to prepare,
15 minutes to cook

**25 g packet fresh mint**
**2 x 175 g (6 oz) salmon fillets**
**240 g (8½ oz) dried pasta
ribbons**

For the salsa

**250 g (9 oz) cherry tomatoes,
halved**
**1 red onion, chopped finely**
**2 garlic cloves, chopped finely**
**½ cucumber, chopped finely**
**2 tablespoons capers, drained
and rinsed**
**1 red chilli, de-seeded and
chopped finely**
**grated zest and juice of a lime**
**1 teaspoon caster sugar**
**salt and freshly ground black
pepper**

*A simple salmon dish that is just bursting with flavour.*

**1** Reserve a couple of mint sprigs and finely chop the rest.

**2** Place the salmon fillets in a wide pan, cover with water and add 1 mint sprig. Bring to the boil and then turn off the heat, leaving the salmon to poach.

**3** Meanwhile, bring a pan of water to the boil, add the pasta and cook according to the packet instructions. Drain and return to the saucepan. Add all the salsa ingredients, together with the chopped mint, and toss together.

**4** Drain the salmon and flake the flesh off the skin, removing any bones. Gently toss the salmon with the pasta and serve garnished with the last mint sprig.

**Variation...** Fillets of rainbow trout would look and taste just as good in this recipe.

# Spicy Italian pasta

Serves 1
**325 calories**
Takes 25 minutes

60 g (2 oz) dried pasta shells
225 g can chopped tomatoes
1 teaspoon tomato purée
½ teaspoon chilli sauce
½ small yellow pepper,
    de-seeded and chopped
    finely
1 celery stick, sliced thinly
1 small courgette, diced
50 g (1¾ oz) small button
    mushrooms, quartered
1 tablespoon shredded fresh
    basil
salt and freshly ground black
    pepper
1 teaspoon grated Parmesan
    cheese, to serve (optional)

*When you want something simple, try this tasty pasta for one – delicious eaten hot or cold.*

**1** Bring a pan of water to the boil, add the pasta and cook for 8–10 minutes until tender, or according to the packet instructions. Drain well.

**2** Meanwhile, place the chopped tomatoes in a saucepan and stir in the tomato purée, chilli sauce, pepper, celery, courgette and mushrooms. Season to taste and bring to the boil. Reduce the heat and simmer for 10 minutes.

**3** Mix the pasta and basil into the tomato sauce. Heat through for 2 minutes and then transfer the mixture to a warmed serving bowl. Scatter with the Parmesan, if using.

**Tip...** If you wish to have this cold, allow it to cool and then pack it into a plastic container with a tightly fitting lid. Keep it in the fridge until you require a portable treat.

# Caribbean meatballs

Serves 4

**198 calories** per serving

Takes 15 minutes to prepare,
30 minutes to cook

**500 g (1 lb 2 oz) lean minced beef**

**25 g packet fresh coriander, chopped finely**

**grated zest and juice of a lime**

**1½ tablespoons Jamaican jerk spices**

**calorie controlled cooking spray**

**1 red pepper, de-seeded and sliced finely**

**½ onion, sliced**

**400 g can chopped tomatoes**

**150 ml (5 fl oz) beef stock**

*Serve with 60 g (2 oz) dried brown rice per person, cooked according to the packet instructions.*

**1** In a large bowl, mix together the mince, coriander, lime zest and juice and 1 tablespoon of jerk spices with your hands. Divide and roll into 20 small balls.

**2** Heat a wide, lidded, non stick pan and spray with the cooking spray. Gently fry the meatballs for 5 minutes, turning until brown all over. You may need to do this in batches. Remove and set aside.

**3** Add the pepper and onion to the pan. Cook for 3–4 minutes until starting to soften. Stir in the chopped tomatoes, beef stock and remaining jerk spices. Return the meatballs. Bring to the boil, cover and simmer for 20 minutes until the meatballs are cooked. Remove the lid and simmer for a further 5–10 minutes until the sauce is thickened. Serve immediately.

# Caribbean chicken casserole

Serves 2

**319 calories** per serving

Takes 15 minutes to prepare,
    25 minutes to cook

**calorie controlled cooking
    spray**

**200 g (7 oz) skinless boneless
    chicken breast, diced**

**½ orange pepper, de-seeded
    and chopped roughly**

**2 teaspoons Caribbean
    seasoning**

**200 g (7 oz) sweet potato,
    peeled and diced**

**½ x 410g can black eyed
    beans, drained and rinsed**

**2 tomatoes, cut into wedges**

**200 ml (7 fl oz) hot chicken
    stock**

**50 g (1¾ oz) frozen sweetcorn**

*This spicy casserole is packed with colourful vegetables
and pulses.*

**1** Heat a lidded non stick saucepan until hot and spray with
the cooking spray. Add the chicken and pepper and brown for
4 minutes. Add the Caribbean seasoning and sweet potato and
cook for 1 minute, stirring.

**2** Mix in the black eyed beans, tomatoes and stock, cover
and simmer for 20 minutes. Add the sweetcorn and cook for a
further 5 minutes. Serve.

# Moroccan aubergine with chick peas

Serves 1
**273 calories**
Takes 22 minutes

calorie controlled cooking
  spray
½ red onion, sliced finely
4 baby aubergines, trimmed
  and halved (see Tip)
2 teaspoons ras el hanout or
  Moroccan spice mix
¼ teaspoon mild chilli powder
1 tablespoon tomato purée
50 g (1¾ oz) spinach, washed
½ x 410 g can chick peas,
  drained and rinsed
1 teaspoon clear honey
grated zest of ½ a small lemon
1 tablespoon chopped fresh
  coriander leaves, to garnish

*Serve this spicy dish with 1 tablespoon of tzatziki and a
60 g (2 oz) griddled flatbread.*

**1** Heat a lidded non stick saucepan and spray with the
cooking spray. Add nearly all the onion (reserving a little
for garnish) and the aubergines. Cook gently for 5 minutes,
covered, until starting to soften. Stir occasionally.

**2** Add the ras el hanout or Moroccan spice mix, chilli powder
and tomato purée and cook for 1 minute. Remove from the
heat and add 6 tablespoons of cold water. Return to a very
low heat and cook gently, covered, for 6 minutes, stirring
occasionally until the aubergine is tender.

**3** Add the spinach, chick peas and a splash of water. Cook for
4 minutes, stirring until the spinach is wilted and the juices
have thickened. Remove from the heat and stir through the
honey and lemon zest. Serve topped with the reserved red
onion and the coriander.

**Tip...** If you can't find baby aubergines, use 175 g (6 oz)
ordinary aubergine, cut into small cubes.

# Thai infused barbecued tuna

Serves 6

**294 calories** per serving

Takes 20 minutes to prepare,
4–6 minutes to cook

**For the tuna**

**1 lime**

**1 red chilli, de-seeded and
diced**

**1 tablespoon grated fresh root
ginger**

**½ x 25 g packet fresh
coriander, chopped**

**1 tablespoon fish sauce**

**6 x 100 g (3½ oz) fresh tuna
steaks**

**calorie controlled cooking
spray**

**freshly ground black pepper**

**For the noodle salad**

**a kettleful of boiling water**

**250 g (9 oz) dried thin rice
noodles**

**2 carrots, peeled and grated
coarsely**

**250 g (9 oz) beansprouts**

**juice of a lime**

**2 tablespoons fish sauce**

*Fresh tuna steaks are ideal to cook on the barbecue as the
firm texture holds together well.*

**1** Preheat the barbecue, giving it time to reach a moderate
heat. Grate the zest from the lime and slice the lime into
wedges. Mix the lime zest, chilli, ginger and coriander with the
fish sauce, seasoning with black pepper. Rub the mixture into
the tuna steaks and leave until ready to barbecue.

**2** Pour boiling water over the rice noodles in a large bowl and
leave to soften for 4 minutes. Drain, rinse in cold water and
then mix together with the grated carrots, beansprouts, lime
juice and fish sauce.

**3** When the barbecue has reached the desired cooking heat,
lightly spray both the barbecue grill rack and the tuna steaks
with the cooking spray. Place the tuna steaks on the grill rack
and barbecue for 2–3 minutes on either side.

**4** Serve with the rice noodle salad, with the lime wedges to
squeeze over the tuna.

**Tip...** If you don't have a barbecue, try cooking the tuna
steaks on a hot griddle pan.

# Kashmiri chicken skewers

Serves 4
**176 calories** per serving
Takes 20 minutes
❄

*Perfect food for sharing. Place bowls of herb salad, chopped tomato and cucumber in the centre of the table. Serve with 60 g (2 oz) dried brown rice per person, cooked according to the packet instructions.*

3 cardamom pods

1 teaspoon coriander seeds

a generous pinch of saffron strands

½ teaspoon ground cinnamon

grated zest and juice of 2 limes

4 x 150 g (5½ oz) skinless boneless chicken breasts, cut into strips

4 tablespoons 0% fat Greek yogurt

salt and freshly ground black pepper

**1** Preheat the grill to medium high. Remove the seeds from the cardamom pods. Using a mortar and pestle, pound the cardamom seeds, coriander seeds and saffron together until crushed.

**2** Transfer the spices to a large bowl and add the cinnamon, juice of both limes, zest of 1 lime and the chicken strips. Toss the chicken to coat in the spices.

**3** Thread the chicken on to skewers and cook under the grill for 5–8 minutes, turning until cooked through.

**4** Meanwhile, mix the yogurt with the remaining lime zest and some seasoning. Set aside. Serve the chicken skewers with the zesty dressing.

# Jamaican black beans

Serves 4

**325 calories** per serving

Takes 50 minutes to prepare +
overnight soaking,
45 minutes to cook

**225 g (8 oz) dried black beans**
**1 bay leaf**
**calorie controlled cooking
spray**
**1 large onion, chopped finely**
**2 garlic cloves, crushed**
**1 teaspoon English mustard**
**1 tablespoon black treacle**
**a small bunch of fresh thyme,
woody stems removed and
leaves chopped**
**1 small red chilli, de-seeded
and chopped finely**
**400 ml (14 fl oz) vegetable
stock**
**1 red pepper, de-seeded and
diced**
**1 yellow pepper, de-seeded
and diced**
**1 kg (2 lb 4 oz) butternut
squash, peeled, de-seeded
and cut into 1 cm (½ inch)
dice**
**salt and freshly ground black
pepper**

*This dish has the vibrant colours of the Caribbean
combined with hot and spicy flavours.*

**1** Place the beans in a bowl, cover with water and leave to
soak overnight. The next day, drain, rinse well and drain again.

**2** Place the beans in a large lidded saucepan or lidded
flameproof casserole dish and cover with water. Add the bay
leaf and bring to the boil. Boil rapidly for 10 minutes, removing
the scum as it collects on the surface with a slotted spoon.
Reduce the heat and simmer, covered, for a further 30 minutes,
until tender. Drain and set aside.

**3** Spray the pan or casserole dish with the cooking spray
and stir-fry the onion and garlic for a few minutes, until
softened, adding a little water if necessary to prevent them
from sticking.

**4** Add all the other ingredients, including the beans, and
stir together. Cover, bring to the boil and then uncover and
simmer for 45 minutes, until all the vegetables are tender and
the sauce thickened. Check the seasoning and serve.

# Persian chicken tagine

Serves 4

**575 calories** per serving

Takes 25 minutes to prepare, 50 minutes to cook

**calorie controlled cooking spray**

**8 skinless chicken thighs**

**1 large onion, chopped**

**4 garlic cloves, crushed**

**1 celery stick, chopped finely**

**2 carrots, peeled and chopped finely**

**1 tablespoon plain white flour**

**½ teaspoon ground cinnamon**

**1 teaspoon ground cumin**

**1 teaspoon turmeric**

**150 ml (5 fl oz) white wine**

**600 ml (20 fl oz) chicken stock**

**2 x 400 g cans chick peas, drained and rinsed**

**a bunch of fresh coriander, chopped**

**salt and freshly ground black pepper**

*A warm cinnamon and cumin flavoured casserole. Serve with 60 g (2 oz) dried rice per person, cooked according to the packet instructions.*

**1** Heat a casserole or large, lidded, heavy-based saucepan and spray with the cooking spray. Add the chicken thighs, season and brown on all sides. Remove and set aside.

**2** Add the onion, garlic, celery and carrots and cook for 10 minutes, until softened, stirring occasionally.

**3** Mix the flour with the spices and stir in, cooking for 2 minutes. Return the chicken thighs to the pan, pour over the wine and stock, season, cover and cook on a low heat for 45 minutes.

**4** Add the chick peas, cook for a further 5 minutes and then sprinkle the coriander over and serve.

# Texan beef chilli

Serves 4

**287 calories** per serving

Takes 10 minutes to prepare,
30 minutes to cook

calorie controlled cooking
  spray

**500 g (1 lb 2 oz) lean minced
  beef**

**2 garlic cloves, crushed**

**1 tablespoon mild or hot chilli
  powder**

**2 tablespoons tomato purée**

**125 ml (4 fl oz) red wine**

**150 ml (5 fl oz) beef stock**

**410 g can kidney beans,
  drained and rinsed**

**6 tablespoons smoky
  barbecue sauce**

*Everyone loves a bowl of spicy chilli. Enjoy with a crisp green salad or put the chilli in two 12 g tacos per person and top with salad leaves and shredded onion.*

**1** Heat a wide non stick saucepan and spray with the cooking spray. Add the mince and cook for 5 minutes, breaking up the meat with a wooden spoon. Add the garlic and chilli powder and cook for 2 minutes.

**2** Stir in the tomato purée, red wine, beef stock, kidney beans and barbecue sauce. Simmer for 30 minutes until thickened. Serve immediately.

**☺ Variation...** For a vegetarian version, use a 350 g packet of vegetarian mince instead of the beef mince and replace the beef stock with vegetable stock.

# Goan prawn curry

Serves 4
**140 calories** per serving
Takes 30 minutes

400 g (14 oz) raw prawns, peeled but tails left on, defrosted if frozen

2 tablespoons white wine vinegar

1 teaspoon turmeric

1 tablespoon coriander seeds

1 teaspoon cumin seeds

calorie controlled cooking spray

1 onion, sliced finely

4 garlic cloves, cut into slivers

2.5 cm (1 inch) fresh root ginger, chopped finely

100 ml (3½ fl oz) reduced fat coconut milk

juice of a lemon

300 ml (10 fl oz) fish or vegetable stock

1 large green chilli, de-seeded and sliced thinly

a bunch of fresh coriander, chopped

salt

*Goa is on the west coast of India, famous for its fantastic seafood cooking. Freshly caught fish and seafood are combined with the usual Indian curry spices and the more usually South East Asian addition of coconut and fresh ginger. Serve with 60 g (2 oz) dried basmati rice per person, cooked according to the packet instructions.*

**1** Place the prawns in a bowl with the vinegar and ½ teaspoon of salt and leave to soak for 5 minutes to enhance their flavour. Meanwhile, grind the turmeric, coriander seeds and cumin seeds together in a mortar and pestle or spice mill until they form a fine powder.

**2** Heat a large non stick frying pan and spray with the cooking spray. Add the onion, garlic and ginger and fry gently for 5 minutes until softened. Stir in the ground spices and fry for 2 minutes more.

**3** Add the coconut milk, lemon juice and stock, bring to the boil and then simmer for 5 minutes. Add the prawns and cook for 3–4 minutes until they have all turned pink. Finally, stir in the chilli and coriander just before serving.

**Variation...** Use 2 tablespoons of curry paste for convenience instead of all or some of the spices.

# Cajun pork steaks with sweet potato chips

Serves 4
**524 calories** per serving
Takes 55 minutes

calorie controlled cooking
spray
1.25 kg (2 lb 12 oz) sweet
potatoes, peeled and cut into
wedges
½ vegetable stock cube,
crumbled
4 x 175 g (6 oz) pork loin
steaks, trimmed of visible fat
juice of a lime
2 teaspoons Cajun spices
grated zest of ½ a lime
½ pineapple, peeled, cored
and chopped finely
½ red pepper, de-seeded and
diced
½ green chilli, de-seeded and
diced

*If you're looking for something different to serve next time
you have friends around for dinner, this recipe will prove
a talking point. The tropical flavours of the salsa perfectly
complement the spicy pork steaks and caramelised sweet
potato chips.*

**1** Preheat the oven to Gas Mark 6/200°C/ fan oven 180°C.
Lightly spray a non stick baking tray with the cooking spray.

**2** Bring a pan of water to the boil, add the sweet potato
wedges and vegetable stock cube and cook for 5 minutes.
Drain the potatoes, spread out on the baking tray and spray
with the cooking spray. Cook in the oven for 25–30 minutes,
turning halfway through.

**3** Meanwhile, place the pork steaks on a plate, drizzle half the
lime juice over them and sprinkle the Cajun spices on both sides
of each steak. Set aside and preheat the grill to medium high.

**4** Mix the remaining lime juice and the lime zest together with
the pineapple, red pepper and chilli in a small serving bowl.

**5** Grill the pork steaks for 12–15 minutes, or until they are
cooked through and the juices run clear. Serve with the sweet
potato chips and the pineapple salsa spooned over the pork.

**Tip...** To prepare a pineapple, first slice off the base and
the leaves of the pineapple. Stand the pineapple upright
and cut into wedges. Trim away the core from each wedge,
and then slice the flesh away from the skin, as if you were
preparing a melon.

# Mexican taco burgers

Serves 4
**397 calories** per serving
Takes 30 minutes
❄ (uncooked burgers only)

**500 g (1 lb 2 oz) lean minced beef**
**1 onion, grated**
**35 g packet Old El Paso Fajita Seasoning Mix**
**1 egg, lightly beaten**
**calorie controlled cooking spray**
**8 tacos**
**1 Little Gem lettuce, shredded**
**3 tomatoes, de-seeded and diced**
**salt and freshly ground black pepper**

For the guacamole
**100 g (3½ oz) avocado flesh**
**1 small garlic clove, crushed**
**juice of ¼ of a lemon**
**2 tablespoons 0% fat Greek yogurt**

*Serve these lightly spiced tacos with a large green salad.*

**1** Preheat the oven to Gas Mark 4/180°C/fan oven 160°C. In a bowl, mix together the mince, onion, fajita seasoning mix and egg. Season and, using wet hands, form into 16 balls. Flatten the tops to make mini burgers.

**2** Heat a large non stick frying pan and spray with the cooking spray. Cook the burgers in two batches for 6–7 minutes each, turning once, until golden and cooked through. Remove and keep warm.

**3** Stand the tacos upright on a baking tray and warm in the oven for 2 minutes.

**4** Meanwhile, to make the guacamole, in a bowl mash together the avocado, garlic, lemon juice and yogurt and season.

**5** To serve, divide the lettuce and tomatoes between the tacos and add two mini burgers and a spoonful of guacamole to each. Serve two tacos per person.

**Variation...** You can swap the minced beef for the same quantity of lean minced turkey.

# Dominican vegetable curry

Serves 2
**230 calories** per serving
Takes 25 minutes

100 g (3½ oz) potato, peeled
and cut into large dice

200 g (7 oz) carrots, peeled
and cut into large dice

100 g (3½ oz) cauliflower
florets

100 g (3½ oz) green beans,
sliced

75 g (2¾ oz) peas, defrosted
if frozen

½ x 200 g jar Keralan curry
paste

salt and freshly ground black
pepper

*This is ideal for those who like mild curries. Serve with
60 g (2 oz) dried basmati rice per person, cooked according
to the packet instructions.*

**1** Bring a large lidded pan of water to the boil, add the potato
and carrots and cook for 10 minutes.

**2** Add the cauliflower and green beans and continue to cook
for another 5 minutes.

**3** Drain the vegetables and return to the pan with the rest of
the ingredients and 100 ml (3½ fl oz) of water. Stir well, bring
to the boil, cover and simmer for 5 minutes.

**Variation...** If you like your curries hot, add some chopped
red chilli when you add the curry paste.

# Family favourites

# Mexican beanburgers

Serves 4
**370 calories** per serving
Takes 20 minutes + 30 minutes chilling ⓥ ❄

*These spicy, Mexican-style beanburgers have a really satisfying texture and a gentle kick.*
*Serve with relish and a big green salad.*

1 tablespoon tomato purée
2 x 400 g cans mixed beans, drained and
  rinsed
1 small onion, chopped roughly
1 garlic clove, chopped
400 g can mixed peppers in brine, drained,
  rinsed and chopped roughly
1 red chilli, de-seeded and chopped finely
1 teaspoon ground cumin

a small bunch of fresh parsley, coriander or
  chives
1 egg, beaten
2 tablespoons plain white flour
calorie controlled cooking spray
salt and freshly ground black pepper

To serve
4 medium burger buns
salad leaves, to serve

**1** Mix the tomato purée to a paste with 1 tablespoon of water and place in a food processor with all the other main ingredients except the flour and cooking spray. Whizz to a rough paste.

**2** Using wet hands, shape the mixture into four burgers. Put the flour on a plate and coat the burgers in it. Refrigerate for 30 minutes to allow them to firm up.

**3** Heat a large non stick frying pan and spray with the cooking spray. Fry the burgers for about 4 minutes on each side until browned and heated through.

**4** Split the buns and fill with the burgers and salad leaves. Serve.

# Spicy spaghetti bolognese

**Serves 4**

**345 calories** per serving

Takes 25 minutes to prepare,
30 minutes to cook

✳

225 g (8 oz) extra lean minced
beef

1 onion, chopped

1 garlic clove, crushed

150 g (5½ oz) mushrooms,
sliced

1 cooking apple, peeled, cored
and grated

150 g (5½ oz) carrots, peeled
and grated

1 teaspoon hot chilli powder
or cayenne pepper

1 teaspoon ground coriander

2 tablespoons tomato purée

400 g can chopped tomatoes

225 g (8 oz) dried spaghetti

salt and freshly ground black
pepper

*We've spiced up this all time favourite with a hint of chilli.*

**1** Heat a large, lidded, non stick frying pan and add the mince. Dry-fry for 5 minutes until it is evenly browned, breaking it up with a wooden spoon if necessary. Add the onion, garlic, mushrooms, apple, carrots, chilli powder or cayenne pepper and ground coriander and cook for a further 5 minutes.

**2** Stir in the tomato purée, tomatoes and 4 tablespoons of water and bring to the boil. Cover, reduce the heat and simmer for 30 minutes, stirring from time to time.

**3** Meanwhile, bring a pan of water to the boil, add the spaghetti and cook for 8–10 minutes until tender, or according to the packet instructions. Drain well.

**4** Mix the spaghetti into the bolognese mixture, season and heat through to serve.

**Tip...** It is important to add some sweetness to a bolognese sauce as tomatoes can be a little acidic. In this recipe the grated apple and carrot add sweetness, using natural fruit sugar rather than ordinary sugar.

❂ **Variation...** For a vegetarian version, use 225 g (8 oz) Quorn mince instead of the beef mince. It doesn't need to be browned first.

# Thai salmon surprise

Serves 4

**255 calories** per serving

Takes 15 minutes to prepare,
25 minutes to cook

❄ (at end of step 3)

1 small onion, chopped finely

2 cm (¾ inch) lemongrass
stalk, chopped finely

2 cm (¾ inch) fresh root
ginger, chopped finely

50 g (1¾ oz) mushrooms,
chopped finely

½ red pepper, de-seeded and
chopped finely

½ teaspoon Thai 7 spice

1 tablespoon tomato purée

1 tablespoon chopped fresh
coriander, plus a few extra
sprigs to garnish

4 x 125 g (4½ oz) thick cut
salmon steaks

4 tablespoons soy sauce

150 ml (5 fl oz) fish or
vegetable stock

salt and freshly ground black
pepper

*This is so tasty. Serve with a green salad or 60 g (2 oz)
dried cooked noodles per person, cooked according to the
packet instructions.*

**1** Dry-fry the onion in a non stick frying pan for 2 minutes.
Add the lemongrass and ginger, stir well and then add the
mushrooms, pepper and Thai 7 spice. Stir and cook over a
low heat for 1 minute.

**2** Remove the pan from the heat and stir in the tomato purée
and chopped coriander. Set aside to cool. (This mixture forms
the salmon 'stuffing'.)

**3** Slice the salmon steaks in half horizontally. Spread a
quarter of the stuffing mix evenly over four steak halves and
then cover with the remaining halves. Preheat the oven to Gas
Mark 4/180°C/fan oven 160°C.

**4** Arrange the steaks in an ovenproof baking dish so that they
fit comfortably. Pour over the soy sauce and stock and season.
Cover with a lid or a piece of foil and bake for 25 minutes.

**5** Serve, garnished with the coriander sprigs.

**Tip...** You can only freeze the salmon if it has not
been previously frozen, so be sure to check with your
fishmonger.

**Variation...** You can also use 2 teaspoons each of
ready-prepared fresh lemongrass and ginger, which are
available in small jars in most large supermarkets.

# Chicken tikka masala

Serves 4
**199 calories** per serving
Takes 40 minutes +
  30 minutes marinating

**200 g (7 oz) low fat natural yogurt**
**2 teaspoons curry powder**
**2 teaspoons tomato purée**
**4 x 125 g (4½ oz) skinless chicken breast fillets, diced**
**salt and freshly ground black pepper**
**2 tablespoons chopped fresh coriander, to serve**

For the sauce
**calorie controlled cooking spray**
**1 onion, chopped finely**
**1 tablespoon curry powder**
**400 g can chopped tomatoes**
**150 ml (5 fl oz) chicken stock**

*Just right for a Friday night. Serve with 60 g (2 oz) dried basmati rice per person, cooked according to the packet instructions.*

**1** Mix the yogurt together with the curry powder, tomato purée and seasoning and then stir in the chicken. Cover and leave to marinate in the fridge for 30 minutes.

**2** Preheat the grill to medium high and place the marinated chicken pieces on the grill rack. Grill for 10–15 minutes until cooked through and lightly charred.

**3** Meanwhile, place a lidded non stick pan over a medium heat and spray with the cooking spray. Cook the onion with 2 tablespoons of water for 5–6 minutes until softened.

**4** Stir in the curry powder, cook for 30 seconds and then add the tomatoes and chicken stock. Simmer briskly for 5 minutes, add the grilled chicken and then simmer for a further 5 minutes.

**5** Top with the coriander just before serving.

# Sweet and spicy pork

Serves 4
**375 calories** per serving
Takes 50 minutes
❄

*Pile this fragrant, sweet casserole on to a bed of steaming couscous and enjoy the sultry heat of the Middle East.*

**1** Heat the oil in a large, lidded, non stick saucepan or flameproof casserole dish. Cook the onion for 5 minutes, until softened and slightly golden.

1 teaspoon olive oil

1 large onion, sliced

2 tablespoons plain white flour

1 teaspoon ground ginger

450 g (1 lb) pork fillet, trimmed of visible fat and sliced into 2 cm (¾ inch) rounds

1 garlic clove, crushed

2 teaspoons harissa

425 ml (15 fl oz) hot vegetable or chicken stock

1 tablespoon tomato purée

6 ready-to-eat apricots, halved

2 tablespoons chopped fresh coriander or sage

salt and freshly ground black pepper

**2** Meanwhile, put the flour and ginger in a plastic bag with the pork. Season, shake well to coat and then remove the meat, shaking off any excess flour. Add the meat to the pan with the garlic and stir-fry over a high heat for 3–4 minutes, until the pork has browned.

**3** Add the harissa and cook for 1 minute before stirring in the stock and tomato purée. Bring to the boil, reduce the heat, cover and simmer gently for 15 minutes. Add the apricots and coriander or sage, season and simmer for a further 10 minutes.

**4** Meanwhile, place the couscous in a bowl with the saffron, if using. Pour the hot stock over and leave for 5 minutes to soak. Stir in the chives with a fork (this will also fluff up the grains) and season to taste.

**5** Spoon the couscous into warmed bowls and pile on the pork. Serve at once.

**For the couscous**

175 g (6 oz) dried couscous

4 saffron strands (optional)

300 ml (10 fl oz) hot vegetable stock

2 tablespoons snipped fresh chives

**Tip...** Harissa is made up of a lively combination of Middle Eastern spices. It adds a great flavour – and heat too.

**Variation...** For a change, replace the harissa with 2 tablespoons of dark soy sauce and a dash of Tabasco sauce.

# Chilli seafood

Serves 4
**100 calories** per serving
Takes 15 minutes

2 tablespoons hoisin sauce
2 tablespoons chilli sauce
1 teaspoon soy sauce
1 teaspoon fish sauce
½ teaspoon caster sugar
½ teaspoon sesame oil
calorie controlled cooking
  spray
5 cm (2 inches) fresh root
  ginger, chopped finely
6 spring onions, chopped, plus
  extra to garnish
2 garlic cloves, crushed
250 g (9 oz) cooked seafood
  selection, defrosted if frozen
½ teaspoon dried chilli flakes

*You could just use prawns for this recipe, but mixed
seafood is easy and convenient. The sauce gives the dish
a good spicy kick. Serve with steamed pak choi and 60 g
(2 oz) dried basmati rice per person, cooked according to
the packet instructions.*

**1** Mix together the first six ingredients in a bowl and set aside.

**2** Heat a wok or large non stick frying pan and spray with the
cooking spray. Stir-fry the ginger, chopped spring onions and
garlic for 1 minute. Add the seafood and chilli flakes and toss
well to mix.

**3** Pour the sauce mixture over and toss again. Serve
immediately, scattered with the extra spring onions.

**Variation...** This recipe is also very good made with
4 x 150 g (5½ oz) sliced, skinless, boneless chicken
breasts instead of the seafood. Stir-fry for 4–5 minutes
until cooked through before adding the ginger, spring
onions and garlic.

# Butternut squash and bean chilli

Serves 4

**240 calories** per serving

Takes 30 minutes to prepare, 30 minutes to cook

*This recipe is wonderfully filling. Serve with a 50 g (1¾ oz) crusty roll per person or try it with 60 g (2 oz) dried couscous or basmati rice per person, cooked according to the packet instructions.*

**1** Preheat the oven to Gas Mark 6/200°C/fan oven 180°C. Place the butternut squash on a non stick baking tray and bake for 20 minutes.

1 butternut squash, peeled, de-seeded and cut into large chunks

calorie controlled cooking spray

2 garlic cloves, chopped

2 red chillies, de-seeded and chopped

420 g can kidney beans, drained and rinsed

300 g can cannellini beans, drained and rinsed

300 g can flageolet beans, drained and rinsed

425 ml (15 fl oz) vegetable stock

a small bunch of fresh coriander, chopped

1 teaspoon cornflour

40 g (1½ oz) half fat mature Cheddar cheese, grated

salt and freshly ground black pepper

**2** Meanwhile, place a 2 litre (3½ pint) lidded flameproof casserole dish on the hob. Spray with the cooking spray and fry the garlic and chillies for half a minute. Add all the beans, the stock, coriander and seasoning and stir together.

**3** Mix the cornflour with a little water to make a paste and then stir it into the bean mixture. Finally add the half baked squash to the casserole dish. Cover and cook in the oven for 20 minutes.

**4** Remove the dish from the oven and sprinkle over the cheese. Return to the oven, uncovered, for a further 10 minutes.

# Rogan josh pasta

Serves 4
**494 calories** per serving
Takes 20 minutes
❄ (lamb sauce only)

**250 g (9 oz) dried tagliatelle**
**a kettleful of boiling water**
**calorie controlled cooking**
    **spray**
**1 onion, chopped finely**
**400 g (14 oz) lean minced**
    **lamb**
**2 tablespoons rogan josh**
    **curry paste**
**300 g (10½ oz) passata**
**175 g (6 oz) cherry tomatoes,**
    **halved**
**2 tablespoons chopped fresh**
    **coriander**

*A fast and fabulous version of a traditional Indian lamb stew, which translated means 'red meat juices'. The rich red colour comes from the chillies in the curry paste.*

**1** Put the tagliatelle in a saucepan and cover with the boiling water. Bring to the boil and simmer for 10–12 minutes until 'al dente', or cook according to the packet instructions.

**2** Meanwhile, heat a lidded non stick saucepan and spray with the cooking spray. Cook the onion for 3 minutes until beginning to soften.

**3** Add the mince and curry paste and cook on high for 1 minute, stirring constantly. Stir in the passata and cherry tomatoes and bring to the boil. Cover and simmer gently for 5 minutes.

**4** Drain the pasta and add to the lamb sauce along with the coriander. Toss to coat and serve immediately.

⊙ **Variation...** For a vegetarian version, replace the minced lamb with a 350 g packet of vegetarian mince.

# Butterflied tandoori chicken

Serves 6
**252 calories** per serving
Takes 20 minutes to prepare
  + marinating,
  1 hour 20 minutes to cook

**1.5 kg (3 lb 5 oz) whole chicken**
**300 g (10½ oz) low fat natural yogurt**
**3 garlic cloves, crushed**
**2.5 cm (1 inch) fresh root ginger, chopped finely**
**1 tablespoon tandoori curry paste**
**1 teaspoon garam masala**
**salt and freshly ground black pepper**

To garnish
**a small bunch of fresh coriander, chopped (optional)**
**2 limes, cut into wedges**

*Serve with 60 g (2 oz) dried basmati rice per person, cooked according to the packet instructions.*

**1** Remove the back bone and ribs from the chicken (see Tip), turn the chicken so it is skin side up and press down firmly on the breastbone with the heel of your hand to flatten it out.

**2** Remove all the skin, wash the bird under cold running water and then pat dry with kitchen towel.

**3** To make the marinade, combine all of the remaining ingredients, except the garnish, in a bowl and then rub all over the chicken both inside and out. Cover and leave it to marinate in the fridge for at least 1 hour and preferably overnight.

**4** Preheat the oven to Gas Mark 6/200°C/fan oven 180°C and thread two 10 cm (4 inch) metal skewers in a criss-cross fashion through the chicken to keep it flat. Arrange the chicken on a wire rack in a roasting tin, spread over some of the marinade and roast for 40 minutes.

**5** Turn the chicken over, spread with more of the marinade and roast for a further 40 minutes until each side is golden brown and just tender. Leave to rest for a few minutes and then remove the skewers. Scatter with the fresh coriander, if using, and serve with lime wedges to squeeze over.

**Tip...** To remove the back bone and ribs of a chicken, use poultry shears or tough kitchen scissors. Cut the chicken along the back down each side of the back bone. Remove the back bone and discard. Snip the wishbone in half, open out the chicken and snip out the ribs.

# Nasi goreng

Serves 4
**430 calories** per serving
Takes 25 minutes

**240 g (8½ oz) dried basmati rice**
**4 teaspoons Indonesian or Thai red curry paste**
**250 g (9 oz) pork fillet, trimmed of visible fat and cut into thin strips**
**200 g (7 oz) cooked peeled prawns, defrosted if frozen**
**1 tablespoon soy sauce**
**200 g (7 oz) frozen petit pois, defrosted**
**2 eggs, beaten**
**a small bunch of fresh coriander, chopped, to garnish**

*Nasi goreng means 'fried rice' in Indonesia, where it is enjoyed as a quick family meal.*

**1** Bring a pan of water to the boil, add the rice and cook according to the packet instructions. Drain, rinse in cold water and drain again.

**2** Heat the curry paste in a wok or large non stick frying pan, add the pork and stir-fry for 4–5 minutes, until cooked through.

**3** Add the prawns, soy sauce, petit pois and rice and stir-fry for 5 minutes. Push everything to one side of the wok or pan and then pour in the eggs. Stir until lightly set like scrambled egg and then stir in the other ingredients.

**4** Scatter with the chopped coriander and serve.

# Spicy spare ribs

Serves 4

**225 calories** per serving

Takes 10 minutes to prepare,
  50–60 minutes to cook

❄

**750 g (1 lb 10 oz) lean pork
  spare ribs, trimmed of
  visible fat**
**1 tablespoon clear honey**
**2 tablespoons tomato purée**
**2 tablespoons lemon juice**
**3 tablespoons soy sauce**
**3 tablespoons oyster sauce**
**1 teaspoon Chinese five spice**
**1 teaspoon hot chilli powder**
**salt and freshly ground black
  pepper**

To garnish
**4 spring onions, sliced finely**
**4 tomatoes, cut into wedges**

*These spare ribs are well worth the effort. Serve with a
mixed salad for a delicious dinner.*

**1** Preheat the oven to Gas Mark 6/200°C/fan oven 180°C.

**2** Put the spare ribs in a large roasting dish. Mix together
the honey, tomato purée, lemon juice, soy sauce, oyster sauce,
Chinese five spice, chilli powder and seasoning. Pour over
the ribs, tossing them to coat in the mixture. Roast for
50–60 minutes until tender.

**3** Serve the spare ribs sprinkled with the sliced spring onions
and garnished with the tomatoes.

# Spicy gammon and bean hot pot

Serves 4

**225 calories** per serving

Takes 10 minutes to prepare,
20–25 minutes to cook

❄

calorie controlled cooking
   spray

350 g (12 oz) lean gammon
   steak, diced

225 g (8 oz) leeks, sliced

225 g (8 oz) carrots, peeled
   and diced

400 g can chopped tomatoes

400 g can mixed beans in
   chilli sauce

150 ml (5 fl oz) apple juice

1 tablespoon wholegrain
   mustard

salt and freshly ground black
   pepper

*There is an extensive range of canned beans and pulses
available today. Try and include them in your cooking as
they make meals more filling.*

**1** Spray a large, lidded, non stick saucepan with the cooking
spray and cook the gammon over a high heat for 2–3 minutes.

**2** Add the remaining ingredients and bring to the boil. Reduce
the heat, cover and simmer for 20–25 minutes, until the leeks
and carrots are cooked. Serve hot.

**Variation...** You may find the apple juice a little too sweet. If
this is the case, use vegetable or chicken stock instead.

# Spicy fish casserole

Serves 4
**320 calories** per serving
Takes 10 minutes to prepare,
 35 minutes to cook
✳

1 tablespoon vegetable oil
1 onion, chopped
3 celery sticks, chopped finely
1 garlic clove, crushed
2 teaspoons ground cumin
1 teaspoon paprika
2 x 400 g cans chopped
 tomatoes
1 tablespoon tomato purée
50 g (1¾ oz) dried long grain
 rice
500 g (1 lb 2 oz) skinless thick
 cod fillet, cut into 4 cm
 (1½ inch) cubes
400 g can chick peas, drained
 and rinsed
3 tablespoons chopped fresh
 coriander
salt and freshly ground black
 pepper
4 tablespoons low fat natural
 yogurt, to garnish

*There's no need to neglect fish during the colder months
– it is readily available and often at its best. Try this great
midweek supper – chunky fish, chick peas and rice,
fragrantly warmed with spices and coriander. All that
is required is a bowlful of fresh green vegetables and a
healthy appetite.*

**1** Heat the oil in a large, lidded, non stick saucepan and cook
the onion and celery gently for 5 minutes. Stir in the garlic and
spices and cook for a further minute.

**2** Stir in the chopped tomatoes, tomato purée and 150 ml
(5 fl oz) of water. Bring to a steady boil and then stir in the rice.
Reduce the heat, cover and simmer gently for 15 minutes.

**3** Add the fish and chick peas and season to taste. Cover
and simmer for a further 10 minutes, until the fish is cooked.
Stir in the coriander, reserving a little to scatter over the top.
Divide the casserole between four warmed plates and top each
with a spoonful of yogurt and a scattering of coriander. Serve
immediately.

**Tip...** Habit often leads us to add the garlic at the same
time as the onion in a recipe. Garlic can burn very quickly
and become bitter tasting, so add it just as the onions are
turning golden and soft.

**Variation...** Replace the fish with 450 g (1 lb) skinless
boneless chicken thighs, adding them at step 1 with the
spices. Stir-fry until lightly coloured and then proceed to
step 2.

# Spicy stuffed tomatoes

Serves 4

**174 calories** per serving

Takes 40 minutes to prepare,
15 minutes to cook

calorie controlled cooking
spray

1 onion, chopped

2 garlic cloves, crushed

450 g (1 lb) potatoes, peeled
and diced

½ teaspoon turmeric

1 teaspoon garam masala

1 teaspoon ground coriander

1½ teaspoons ground cumin

100 g (3½ oz) frozen peas

a small bunch of fresh
coriander, chopped

8 large tomatoes (total weight
about 1 kg/2 lb 4 oz)

salt and freshly ground black
pepper

2 tablespoons low fat natural
yogurt, to serve

*This Middle Eastern-style stuffed tomato dish can be
served with a green salad.*

**1** Preheat the oven to Gas Mark 6/200°C/fan oven 180°C.
Heat a lidded non stick frying pan and spray with the cooking
spray. Add the onion and garlic and fry for 2–3 minutes, until
softened.

**2** Add the potatoes and spices and stir-fry for 1 minute.
Add 300 ml (10 fl oz) of water, bring to the boil and simmer,
covered, for 10 minutes. Remove the lid and simmer for
a further 5 minutes. Add the peas and simmer until the
potatoes are cooked. Stir in the coriander and season.

**3** Slice off the tops and core the tomatoes. Scoop out the
insides with a teaspoon or grapefruit knife and discard.

**4** Put the tomato shells on a baking tray, fill with the potato
mixture and replace the tops. Bake for 15 minutes and serve
hot with ½ tablespoon of yogurt each.

# Turkey patties with chilli apple sauce

Serves 4

**263 calories** per serving

Takes 45 minutes +
  30 minutes chilling

❄ (patties only, before
  cooking)

**For the patties**

**75 g (2¾ oz) fresh wholemeal
  breadcrumbs**

**3 tablespoons skimmed milk**

**1 small onion, grated**

**1 teaspoon dried sage**

**1 small dessert apple, cored
  and diced finely**

**500 g (1 lb 2 oz) lean minced
  turkey**

**calorie controlled cooking
  spray**

**1 tablespoon plain wholemeal
  flour**

**For the sauce**

**1 red chilli, de-seeded and
  diced**

**2 cooking apples, peeled,
  cored and chopped**

**1 tablespoon granulated sugar**

*These tasty patties make a delicious meal. Serve them with
a crunchy salad.*

**1** Combine the breadcrumbs and milk in a mixing bowl and
mix in the onion, sage, diced apple and mince. Using wet
hands, carefully shape into 12 patties. Cover and chill in the
fridge for 30 minutes. Preheat the oven to Gas Mark 5/190°C/
fan oven 170°C.

**2** Meanwhile, make the sauce. Place the chilli, chopped
apples and 2 tablespoons of water in a lidded non stick
saucepan. Cover and cook gently for 10 minutes, stirring
occasionally, until the apples have softened to a purée.
Remove from the heat and stir in the sugar.

**3** Lightly spray a non stick frying pan with the cooking spray.
Dip the turkey patties in the flour to lightly coat them and
brown for 1 minute on each side. Transfer to a non stick baking
tray sprayed with the cooking spray and bake for 20 minutes.
Serve with the chilli apple sauce.

**Tips...** You can make up these patties earlier in the day and
leave them to chill in the fridge, ready for supper.

To make breadcrumbs, let the bread dry out for 30 minutes
on a wire rack and then tear into rough pieces and place in
a food processor or mini blender to make crumbs. Adding
breadcrumbs to the mixture gives a much better texture
and makes the meat go further.

# Red and green pepper burritos

Serves 4
**255 calories** per serving
Takes 35 minutes

calorie controlled cooking
  spray
1 large onion, sliced
½ teaspoon chilli powder
1 red pepper, de-seeded and
  sliced
1 green pepper, de-seeded and
  sliced
100 g (3½ oz) canned kidney
  beans, drained and rinsed
4 soft flour tortillas
100 g (3½ oz) low fat natural
  yogurt
75 g (2¾ oz) half fat Cheddar
  cheese, grated

*A delicious vegetarian version of this popular Mexican
dish. Serve with a crunchy green salad.*

**1** Spray a large non stick frying pan with the cooking spray,
add the onion and sauté for 2–3 minutes on a gentle heat.

**2** Add the chilli powder and stir well before adding the red
and green peppers. Cook for another 8–10 minutes, stirring
occasionally until the peppers have softened and the onion is
starting to caramelise slightly. Add the kidney beans and cook
for 3–4 minutes.

**3** Preheat the grill. Heat the flour tortillas according to the
packet instructions.

**4** Divide the yogurt between the tortillas, spreading it over
the centre of each one. Divide the pepper mixture between
the tortillas, wrap or fold each one and place in a shallow
flameproof dish.

**5** Sprinkle the burritos with the grated cheese and place
under the grill until the cheese is bubbling and melted.

# Spiced beef casserole

Serves 4

**354 calories** per serving

Takes 30 minutes to prepare,
1½ hours to cook

❄

**600 g (1 lb 5 oz) lean braising
steak, cubed**

**calorie controlled cooking
spray**

**1 onion, cut into thin wedges**

**1 red chilli, de-seeded and
sliced thinly**

**2 carrots, peeled and cut into
small chunks**

**350 g (12 oz) parsnips, peeled
and cut into small chunks**

**2 star anise**

**5 whole cloves**

**1 cinnamon stick**

**1 tablespoon plain white flour**

**125 ml (4 fl oz) dry sherry**

**450 ml (16 fl oz) beef stock**

**salt and freshly ground black
pepper**

*This winter warmer has a wonderful chilli kick and is
great served with 60 g (2 oz) dried brown rice per person,
cooked according to the packet instructions, and steamed
green beans.*

**1** Preheat the oven to Gas Mark 3/160°C/fan oven 140°C. Heat
a large, lidded, flame and ovenproof casserole dish and spray
the beef with the cooking spray. Cook the beef for 5 minutes,
turning until brown all over. You will need to do this in batches.
Remove the beef from the dish and set aside.

**2** Spray the casserole dish again with the cooking spray and
add the onion, chilli, carrots, parsnips, star anise, cloves and
cinnamon stick. Cook for 5–8 minutes until starting to brown.
Sprinkle over the flour and stir for 30 seconds.

**3** Return the beef to the pan and pour in the sherry and
beef stock. Bring to the boil, cover and cook in the oven
for 1½ hours until tender and the juices have reduced and
thickened. Check the seasoning, discard the star anise, cloves
and cinnamon stick and serve immediately.

# Speedy suppers

# Tangy duck and plum stir-fry

Serves 2
**344 calories** per serving
Takes 20 minutes

**200 g (7 oz) skinless mini duck fillets**

**calorie controlled cooking spray**

**2 garlic cloves, sliced**

**1 small red chilli, de-seeded and sliced finely**

**1 red onion, cut into thin wedges**

**100 g (3½ oz) small broccoli florets, cut in half if large**

**50 g (1¾ oz) curly leaf kale, chopped**

**50 g (1¾ oz) beansprouts**

**2 tablespoons sake or Japanese rice wine (optional)**

**100 g (3½ oz) plum sauce**

**juice of an orange**

*Curly leaf kale works really well in this stir-fry, but you can use any type of greens such as spinach or Savoy cabbage. Look out for bags of baby leaf greens that are bursting with flavour. Serve with 50 g (1¾ oz) dried egg noodles per person, cooked according to the packet instructions.*

**1** Heat a wok or non stick frying pan until very hot. Spray the duck fillets with the cooking spray and cook for 2 minutes, stirring until starting to brown. Add the garlic, chilli, onion and broccoli and continue to stir-fry for 3 minutes.

**2** Stir in the curly leaf kale and beansprouts and continue to cook for 5 minutes until wilted and tender. Add the sake, if using, and bubble for a few seconds and then stir in the plum sauce, orange juice and 3 tablespoons of cold water. Literally bubble for about 1 minute until thickened slightly. Serve immediately.

# Chilli and ginger glazed cod

Serves 2
**205 calories** per serving
Takes 15 minutes

1 tablespoon cornflour

2 tablespoons light soy sauce

15 g (½ oz) fresh root ginger,
  shredded

1 tablespoon caster sugar

1 red chilli, de-seeded and
  sliced finely

2 teaspoons fish sauce

4 tablespoons white wine
  vinegar

300 g (10½ oz) skinless cod
  loin fillets, cut into chunks

calorie controlled cooking
  spray

To garnish
1 tablespoon fresh mint leaves
2 tablespoons fresh coriander

*This is ideal with 60 g (2 oz) dried brown rice per person,
cooked according to the packet instructions, and stir-fried
vegetables.*

**1** Dissolve 1 teaspoon of cornflour in the soy sauce and set
aside. Put the ginger, sugar, chilli, fish sauce, vinegar and
200 ml (7 fl oz) of water in a small pan. Bring to the boil and
bubble rapidly for 3–4 minutes. Stir in the soy sauce mixture
and bubble for 1 minute more until thickened.

**2** Meanwhile, coat the cod chunks in the remaining cornflour.
Heat a non stick frying pan until hot and spray with the cooking
spray. Cook the cod fillets for 5 minutes until golden and
crispy, turning halfway through. Divide the cod between two
serving bowls, pour over the sauce and top with the mint and
coriander.

**Variation...** Try using 2 x 165 g (5¾ oz) diced, skinless,
boneless chicken breasts instead of the cod.

# Mushroom pilau

**Serves 2**

**285 calories** per serving

Takes 10 minutes to prepare,
15 minutes to cook

1 onion, chopped finely

1 teaspoon sunflower oil

200 g (7 oz) button
mushrooms, quartered

1 teaspoon hot curry powder

½ teaspoon cumin seeds

½ teaspoon black mustard
seeds

125 g (4½ oz) dried basmati
rice

300 ml (10 fl oz) boiling water

*This is a quick and easy vegetable pilau that can be served
on its own or with another curry.*

**1** Heat a lidded non stick pan and cook the onion in the oil
for 3 minutes. Add the mushrooms and cook for a further
3 minutes. Stir in the spices and rice and cook, stirring, for
1 minute.

**2** Add the water, bring to the boil, stir once and then cover the
pan and cook on a very low heat for 15 minutes, without lifting
the lid.

**3** Fluff up the rice with a fork before serving.

**Variation...** For a mushroom and pea pilau, add 100 g
(3½ oz) frozen peas with the rice.

# Piri piri stir-fry beef

Serves 2
**232 calories** per serving
Takes 15 minutes

calorie controlled cooking
  spray
**200 g (7 oz) lean rump steak,
  cut into thin strips**
**2 garlic cloves, sliced**
**2 large red chillies, de-seeded
  and chopped finely**
**1 teaspoon paprika**
**300 g packet fresh mixed
  stir-fry vegetables**
**100 g (3½ oz) passata with
  onion and garlic**
**Juice of ½ a lemon**

*The fiery food of Mozambique uses piri piri, meaning chilli,
as the main spice. Serve with 60 g (2 oz) dried brown rice
per person, cooked according to the packet instructions.*

**1** Heat a wok or non stick frying pan until very hot and spray
with the cooking spray. Add the beef and stir-fry for 2 minutes,
stirring constantly.

**2** Add the garlic and chillies and cook for a further minute,
stirring. Add the paprika and stir-fry vegetables and cook for
2 minutes, stirring constantly.

**3** Pour in the passata and 100 ml (3½ fl oz) of cold water.
Bubble for 1–2 minutes until just thickened.

**4** Squeeze over the lemon juice and serve immediately.

Ⓥ **Variation...** For a vegetarian version, use 200 g (7 oz)
Quorn Steak Strips instead of the beef.

# Spicy stir-fried prawns

Serves 4
**75 calories** per serving
Takes 15 minutes

**200 g (7 oz) mange tout or
sugar snap peas**
**1 large red chilli, de-seeded
and sliced thinly**
**1 large garlic clove, chopped**
**calorie controlled cooking
spray**
**200 g (7 oz) cooked peeled
prawns, defrosted if frozen**
**1 teaspoon ground cumin**
**1 teaspoon ground coriander**
**½ teaspoon ground ginger**
**1 tablespoon soy sauce or fish
sauce**
**2 tablespoons chopped fresh
coriander or parsley**
**juice of a lime**
**salt and freshly ground black
pepper**

*Prawns teamed with crunchy mange tout or sugar snap
peas make a winning combination. This stir-fry makes a
simple and satisfying starter.*

**1** Place the mange tout or sugar snap peas, chilli and garlic
in a non stick frying pan and spray them with the cooking
spray. Heat until sizzling and then add 3 tablespoons of water.
Cook, stirring, for about 3 minutes until the vegetables have
softened.

**2** Mix in the prawns and spices and stir-fry for 2 minutes. Add
the soy sauce or fish sauce, herbs and lime juice. Check the
seasoning and serve.

# Mexican rice

Serves 4
**305 calories** per serving
Takes 25 minutes

calorie controlled cooking
  spray
1 teaspoon cumin seeds
2 red onions, chopped finely
3 garlic cloves, crushed
2 small red chillies, de-seeded
  and chopped finely
300 g (10½ oz) dried long
  grain rice
2 red or orange peppers,
  de-seeded and diced finely
600 ml (20 fl oz) hot vegetable
  stock
1 tablespoon Worcestershire
  sauce
1 tablespoon tomato purée
100 g (3½ oz) frozen peas
100 g (3½ oz) salami, sliced
  into strips
250 g (9 oz) cherry tomatoes,
  halved
a small bunch of fresh
  coriander, chopped
salt and freshly ground black
  pepper

*Hot and fiery, this dish will put you in the mood for a fiesta.*

**1** Heat a large, lidded, non stick saucepan and spray with the cooking spray. Fry the cumin seeds until they start to pop. Add the onions and garlic and a tablespoon of water and stir-fry for a few minutes, until golden and softened.

**2** Add the chillies, rice, peppers, stock, Worcestershire sauce and tomato purée and stir together. Cover the pan and simmer on a low heat for 10–15 minutes, until the rice is very nearly cooked.

**3** Add the peas, cover again and cook for 2 minutes. Now add the salami and tomatoes and stir through. Season and scatter with the fresh coriander before serving.

# Monkfish curry

Serves 4
**215 calories** per serving
Takes 25 minutes

*Serve with 60 g (2 oz) dried basmati rice per person,*
*cooked according to the packet instructions, to soak up*
*the soupy coconut sauce.*

**calorie controlled cooking**
**spray**
**2 onions, diced finely**
**900 g (2 lb) skinless boneless**
**monkfish tail, cut into**
**chunks**
**100 ml (3½ fl oz) reduced fat**
**coconut milk**
**300 ml (10 fl oz) skimmed milk**
**225 g (8 oz) spinach, washed**
**a bunch of fresh coriander,**
**chopped**

For the curry paste
**2 dried kaffir lime leaves or**
**grated zest of 2 limes**
**2 tablespoons boiling water**
**(optional)**
**6 garlic cloves**
**6 cm (2½ inches) fresh root**
**ginger**
**1 red chilli, de-seeded**
**1 teaspoon ground star anise**
**1 teaspoon fennel seeds**
**salt and freshly ground black**
**pepper**

**1** If using dried lime leaves, soak in the boiling water for
5 minutes and then drain and chop. Put all the ingredients
for the curry paste into a food processor, including the lime
leaves or lime zest, and blend to a fine paste. Alternatively
pulverise in a mortar and pestle.

**2** Heat a non stick frying pan and spray with the cooking spray.
Add the onions and fry for 2 minutes and then add the fish and
fry, stirring, for 2 minutes until sealed and white all over.

**3** Add the curry paste and stir to cover all the fish. Add the
coconut milk and skimmed milk, bring to a rapid simmer and
then add the spinach and cook for 5 minutes until the fish is
just cooked through. Do not boil. Check the seasoning, sprinkle
over the chopped coriander and serve.

**Variations...** For a quick alternative, use 2 tablespoons of
Thai curry paste instead of all the individual curry paste
ingredients.

Monkfish is the best fish for this dish as it is so firm and
chunky, but it can be expensive. Cod and salmon make
good alternatives, but take care not to overcook them.

# Thai chicken and spinach curry

Serves 2
**265 calories** per serving
Takes 25 minutes
❄

calorie controlled cooking
spray
**285 g (10 oz)** skinless
boneless chicken breast,
diced
**2 tablespoons** Thai green
curry paste
**250 ml (9 fl oz)** chicken or
vegetable stock
**6 tablespoons** reduced fat
coconut milk
**6 baby corn**, halved
lengthways
**1 small red pepper**, de-seeded
and sliced thinly
**110 g (4 oz)** baby spinach,
washed
**3 tablespoons** chopped fresh
coriander
salt and freshly ground black
pepper

*This Thai-flavoured curry uses a ready-made paste to save time.*

**1** Spray a lidded non stick saucepan with the cooking spray. Add the chicken and stir-fry for 5 minutes until it is golden all over.

**2** Stir in the curry paste and cook, stirring constantly, for 1 minute. Pour over the stock and coconut milk and bring to the boil. Reduce the heat and simmer, covered, for 6 minutes.

**3** Add the baby corn and red pepper. Stir until they are coated in the sauce, cover with the lid and cook for 3 minutes. Add the spinach, stir well, and cook for another 2 minutes over a low heat until the leaves have wilted.

**4** Stir in the coriander and season to taste before serving.

# Pasta arrabbiata

Serves 4
**357 calories** per serving
Takes 20 minutes
❄ (sauce only)

**250 g (9 oz) dried penne**
**calorie controlled cooking spray**
**4 rashers lean back bacon, cut into thin strips**
**2 red onions, sliced**
**2 garlic cloves, crushed**
**1 red chilli, de-seeded and diced**
**2 x 400 g cans chopped tomatoes**
**2 tablespoons tomato purée**
**2 tablespoons fresh basil leaves, torn, plus extra to garnish**
**salt and freshly ground black pepper**

*A classic for a good reason – easy to prepare and tasty too.*

**1** Bring a large pan of water to the boil, add the pasta and cook for 10–12 minutes or according to the packet instructions. Drain and rinse thoroughly.

**2** Meanwhile, spray a large non stick pan with the cooking spray. Add the bacon, onions, garlic and chilli and cook, stirring, over a medium heat for 5 minutes until the onions have softened. Add the chopped tomatoes and tomato purée and cook for 5 minutes until thickened slightly.

**3** Add the basil and season. Add the drained pasta and stir to combine. Heat until piping hot and serve garnished with the extra basil leaves.

# Moroccan chicken pilaff

Serves 4
**398 calories** per serving
Takes 30 minutes
❄

240 g (8½ oz) dried brown
  basmati rice

140 g (5 oz) fine green beans,
  halved

calorie controlled cooking
  spray

375 g (13 oz) skinless
  boneless chicken breast, cut
  into bite size pieces

1 onion, chopped

2 carrots, peeled and diced

2 teaspoons ras el hanout

200 g can chick peas, drained
  and rinsed

125 g (4½ oz) canned peach
  slices in natural juice,
  drained, reserving
  2 tablespoons juice

juice of a lime

35 g packet fresh coriander,
  chopped

salt and freshly ground black
  pepper

*Ras el hanout is a traditional North African spice mixture.*
*It can be found in larger supermarkets or you could swap it*
*for a Moroccan spice mix.*

**1** Bring a pan of water to the boil, add the rice and cook
according to the packet instructions. Drain.

**2** Meanwhile, bring another pan of water to the boil, add the
green beans and cook for 4–5 minutes or until tender. Drain.

**3** Heat a wok or large non stick frying pan and spray with the
cooking spray. Stir-fry the chicken for 4 minutes until golden
and then remove from the pan and keep warm.

**4** Add the onion, carrots and green beans to the pan and
stir-fry for 7 minutes. Add the ras el hanout, chick peas and
cooked rice and heat through, stirring continuously, for
2 minutes. Stir in the chicken, peaches, peach juice and lime
juice. Season and cook for another 3 minutes. Stir in the
coriander before serving.

**Tip...** You can cook the rice in vegetable stock instead of
water to give it extra flavour.

# Spiced cauliflower pasta

Serves 4
**395 calories** per serving
Takes 25 minutes

1 large cauliflower, cut into
  florets
2 tablespoons ground cumin
1 tablespoon ground
  cinnamon
350 g (12 oz) dried pasta
300 g (10½ oz) low fat natural
  yogurt
25 g packet fresh coriander or
  mint, chopped finely
salt and freshly ground black
  pepper

*This is a very unusual way to cook cauliflower, but once you've tried it you'll make it again and again.*

**1** Preheat the oven to Gas Mark 8/230°C/fan oven 210°C. On a non stick baking tray, toss the cauliflower florets in the cumin and cinnamon. Roast in the oven for 20 minutes or until softened and slightly charred.

**2** Meanwhile, bring a pan of water to the boil, add the pasta and cook according to the packet instructions. Drain.

**3** Toss the pasta with the cooked cauliflower and stir in the yogurt, coriander or mint and seasoning. Serve immediately.

# Lamb jalfrezi

Serves 4

**264 calories** per serving

Takes 15 minutes to prepare,
10 minutes to cook

❄

**calorie controlled cooking spray**

**500 g (1 lb 2 oz) lean lamb leg steak, trimmed of visible fat and cut into strips**

**1 large onion, sliced**

**1 red pepper, de-seeded and sliced**

**1 green pepper, de-seeded and sliced**

**2 tablespoons Madras curry paste**

**400 g can chopped tomatoes**

**2 tablespoons tomato purée**

**100 g (3½ oz) low fat natural yogurt**

*This dish is a very popular choice on restaurant menus throughout the UK. Serve with 60 g (2 oz) dried basmati rice per person, cooked according to the packet instructions.*

**1** Place a large non stick frying pan on the hob to heat. Spray with the cooking spray and fry the lamb strips until lightly browned. Remove them to a plate.

**2** Brown the onion and peppers for 5 minutes over a medium heat and then return the lamb to the pan. Stir in the curry paste and fry for 30 seconds before adding the tomatoes and tomato purée. Gradually stir in the yogurt and then add 150 ml (5 fl oz) of hot water. Bring to the boil and simmer for 10 minutes until the meat and vegetables are tender.

**Variation...** Use the same amount of skinless boneless turkey breast strips in place of the lamb.

# Chorizo and courgette lumache

Serves 4
**299 calories** per serving
Takes 25 minutes

225 g (8 oz) dried lumache or any other shell pasta
2 courgettes, sliced into ribbons
110 g (4 oz) chorizo sausage, cut into 2.5 cm (1 inch) dice
200 g (7 oz) field or flat mushrooms, sliced
400 g can chopped tomatoes
2 tablespoons tomato purée
2 teaspoons Tabasco sauce

*Spicy chorizo sausage complements the creamy courgettes perfectly.*

**1** Bring a large pan of water to the boil, add the pasta and cook for 10–12 minutes or according to the packet instructions, adding the courgette ribbons for the final 2 minutes of cooking. Drain and rinse thoroughly.

**2** Heat a large heavy based frying pan until hot, add the chorizo sausage and dry-fry for 3 minutes until the fat begins to run. Add the mushrooms and stir-fry over a medium heat for 5 minutes. Add the chopped tomatoes and tomato purée, bring to the boil and simmer for 5 minutes until thickened slightly. Stir in the Tabasco sauce.

**3** Add the sauce to the pasta and cook for 2 minutes until heated through. Serve.

**Tip...** An easy way to create courgette ribbons is to cut long, thin pieces along the length of the courgette with a potato or vegetable peeler.

# Chilli crab linguine

Serves 4
**288 calories** per serving
Takes 15 minutes

**250 g (9 oz) dried linguine**
**calorie controlled cooking
    spray**
**25 g packet fresh coriander,
    stalks chopped finely and
    leaves torn up roughly**
**1 green chilli, de-seeded and
    diced**
**2 teaspoons grated fresh root
    ginger**
**400 g can chopped tomatoes**
**2 x 170 g cans white crab
    meat, drained**
**freshly ground black pepper**

*This lightly spiced dish is a fusion of flavours and cuisines.
The aromatic ginger and coriander complement the
sweetness of the crab beautifully.*

**1** Bring a pan of water to the boil, add the pasta and cook
for 10–12 minutes until tender, or according to the packet
instructions. Drain.

**2** Meanwhile, heat a non stick saucepan, spray with the
cooking spray and gently fry the coriander stalks, chilli and
ginger for 1 minute to release the flavours. Tip in the tomatoes
and season with black pepper. Simmer for 8 minutes. Stir in
half the crab meat and then toss with the pasta.

**3** Divide between four warmed bowls and top with the rest of
the crab meat. Scatter generously with the coriander leaves
and serve.

# Tandoori paneer and vegetable biryani

Serves 2
**389 calories** per serving
Takes 23 minutes

1 tablespoon tandoori spice mix

150 g (5½ oz) paneer cheese, cubed

grated zest of a lime

calorie controlled cooking spray

½ onion, diced

½ cauliflower, cut into small florets

1 carrot, peeled and diced

125 g (4½ oz) dried basmati rice

300 ml (10 fl oz) boiling hot vegetable stock

75 g (2¾ oz) cherry tomatoes, halved

75 g (2¾ oz) fine green beans, chopped into small pieces

2 tablespoons chopped fresh coriander, to garnish

*Serve each biryani with 1 tablespoon low fat natural yogurt mixed with ½ teaspoon mint sauce per person, and a sliced red onion and cucumber salad.*

**1** In a bowl, mix together the tandoori spices, paneer cubes and lime zest. Heat a deep, wide, lidded, non stick frying pan and spray with the cooking spray. Remove the paneer from the bowl and reserve the excess spices. Add the paneer to the frying pan and cook for 3 minutes until lightly golden. Remove and set aside.

**2** Spray the pan again with the cooking spray and cook the onion, cauliflower and carrot for 5 minutes until starting to soften. Stir in the reserved spices and rice and cook for 30 seconds. Pour in the stock, cover and simmer for 5 minutes.

**3** Add the tomatoes, beans and the cooked paneer. Cover and cook for a further 5 minutes until the rice is tender. Stir to combine everything and then scatter over the coriander and serve.

**Variation...** For meat eaters, replace the paneer cheese with 300 g (10½ oz) diced, skinless, boneless chicken breasts and cook as in step 1 for 4–5 minutes, making sure the chicken is cooked through.

# Cajun-style beef with herby rice

Serves 2
**383 calories** per serving
Takes 25 minutes

60 g (2 oz) dried basmati rice
2 x 125 g (4½ oz) lean fillet
   steaks, trimmed of visible fat
1 teaspoon Cajun spice mix
calorie controlled cooking
   spray
2 spring onions, sliced finely
2 tablespoons chopped fresh
   coriander
215 g can kidney beans,
   drained and rinsed
grated zest and juice of a lime
salt and freshly ground black
   pepper

*Enjoy with 1 tablespoon reduced fat soured cream and
1 tablespoon reduced fat guacamole per person.*

**1** Bring a pan of water to the boil, add the rice and cook for
10–12 minutes or according to the packet instructions.

**2** Meanwhile, preheat the grill to medium high. Season the
steaks and then rub them all over with the Cajun spice mix.
Spray the steaks with the cooking spray, put on a foil-lined
grill tray and cook for 3–5 minutes on each side or until
cooked to your liking. Transfer to a board, cover with foil and
leave to rest for 5 minutes.

**3** Drain the rice and return to the pan. Stir in the spring
onions, coriander, kidney beans, lime zest and lime juice.
Serve the steak on top of the rice.

# Turkey jambalaya

Serves 4

**470 calories** per serving

Takes 10 minutes to prepare,
15 minutes to cook

1 tablespoon vegetable oil

1 red (or ordinary) onion,
chopped finely

2 celery sticks, chopped

2 garlic cloves, crushed

350 g (12 oz) skinless
boneless turkey breast, cut
into chunks

1 large green pepper,
de-seeded and chopped

100 g (3½ oz) button
mushrooms

4 tomatoes, skinned and
chopped

350 g (12 oz) cooked long
grain rice

2 tablespoons chopped fresh
parsley

2–3 teaspoons Cajun spice
mix

½ teaspoon chilli powder
(optional)

salt and freshly ground black
pepper

*If you can't find a Cajun spice mix, try using a combination
of paprika and dried thyme instead.*

**1** Heat the oil in a non stick frying pan and sauté the onion,
celery and garlic until softened, about 2–3 minutes. Add the
turkey and cook for 3–4 more minutes.

**2** Add the pepper, mushrooms and tomatoes and continue to
cook for 2–3 minutes, stirring often.

**3** Stir in the cooked rice, parsley, Cajun spice mix and
chilli powder, if using. Cook for 6–8 more minutes, stirring
frequently until the turkey is cooked.

**4** Check the seasoning, adding a little more chilli powder if
desired. Spoon on to warm plates and serve at once.

Something special

# Jalapeño steak

Serves 2
**325 calories** per serving
Takes 30 minutes

**200 g (7 oz) baby new potatoes, scrubbed and sliced thinly**
**calorie controlled cooking spray**
**2 shallots, chopped finely**
**25 g (1 oz) jalapeño peppers from a jar, drained**
**5 tablespoons barbecue sauce**
**2 tablespoons tomato ketchup**
**2 x 110 g (4 oz) lean fillet steaks, trimmed of visible fat**
**a generous pinch of paprika**

*Serve with blanched asparagus spears and sliced runner beans.*

**1** Preheat the oven to Gas Mark 6/200°C/fan oven 180°C. Put the potatoes on a non stick baking tray and spray with the cooking spray. Bake in the oven for 20 minutes until golden and crispy.

**2** Meanwhile, heat a non stick frying pan until hot, spray with the cooking spray and gently cook the shallots for 3–4 minutes until softened. Remove from the heat and transfer to a jug suitable for a hand blender. Add the jalapeño peppers, barbecue sauce, tomato ketchup and 4 tablespoons of cold water. Whizz until smooth.

**3** Heat the frying pan again until hot and spray again with the cooking spray. Cook the steaks for 3 minutes on each side or until cooked to your liking. Transfer to a plate and loosely cover with foil. Set aside.

**4** Pour the barbecue sauce into the steak pan, simmer for 1–2 minutes and then return the steaks, turning to coat.

**5** Season the potatoes with the paprika and serve with the steak and sauce.

# Caribbean cod

Serves 4
**200 calories** per serving
Takes 20 minutes

**4 x 150 g (5½ oz) skinless cod steaks or fillets**
**1 teaspoon olive oil**

For the salsa
**1 small red onion, chopped finely**
**1 green chilli, de-seeded and chopped finely**
**1 red pepper, de-seeded and diced**
**a handful of fresh basil leaves, chopped finely**
**juice of 2 limes**
**2 tomatoes, de-seeded and chopped finely**
**2 fresh pineapple slices, peeled, cored and diced**

*Plain grilled cod is turned into a lovely meal with the addition of a spicy, fresh salsa.*

**1** Make the salsa by combining all the ingredients in a bowl. Cover and leave to one side. (If you do this in a food processor, do not over process or you will lose the chunky texture of the salsa.)

**2** Preheat the grill to medium.

**3** Brush the cod steaks with a little oil and grill for 3–4 minutes on each side, or until just cooked through. Spoon the salsa over the cod and serve immediately.

# Spicy spinach cannelloni

Serves 4

**267 calories** per serving

Takes 15 minutes to prepare,
35–40 minutes to cook

**400 g can chopped tomatoes
with onion and herbs**

**100 ml (3½ fl oz) vegetable
stock**

**250 g (9 oz) Quark**

**1 egg yolk**

**1 red chilli, de-seeded and
chopped finely**

**375 g (13 oz) frozen spinach,
defrosted**

**150 g (5½ oz) low fat soft
cheese with garlic and herbs**

**½ teaspoon cayenne pepper**

**125 g (4½ oz) dried cannelloni
tubes (about 12)**

**2 tablespoons roughly
chopped fresh coriander, to
serve**

*Turn up the heat with this classic dish by adding piquant
cayenne pepper. If you prefer less heat, use mild chilli
powder instead.*

**1** Preheat the oven to Gas Mark 6/200°C/fan oven 180°C. In a
jug, mix together the tomatoes and vegetable stock. Set aside.
In a bowl, mix together the Quark, egg yolk and chilli and set
aside.

**2** Squeeze out the excess water from the spinach and put into
a large bowl. Mix with the soft cheese and cayenne pepper.
Using a piping bag and a 2 cm (¾ inch) nozzle, pipe the
mixture into the cannelloni tubes and arrange in an 1.75 litre
(3 pint) ovenproof dish. Pour over the tomato sauce.

**3** Dollop the Quark mixture over the top. With the back of a
spoon, spread the mixture to join up the dollops. It doesn't
matter if the tomato sauce marbles a little with the Quark. Bake
in the oven for 35–40 minutes until golden and the pasta is
cooked. Scatter over the coriander and serve immediately.

**Tip...** If you don't have a piping bag, use a teaspoon to
stuff the cannelloni – it will just take a little bit longer.

# Chicken Kashmiri

Serves 4
**270 calories** per serving
Takes 45 minutes ❄

*Meltingly tender and moist chicken pieces in an aromatic and spicy yogurt sauce. Serve with 60 g (2 oz) dried basmati rice per person, cooked according to the packet instructions.*

calorie controlled cooking spray

4 x 150 g (5½ oz) skinless boneless chicken breasts, cubed

200 g (7 oz) small new potatoes, scrubbed and quartered

1 onion, chopped finely

4 garlic cloves, crushed

5 cm (2 inches) fresh root ginger, chopped finely

2 cardamom pods, seeds only

½ teaspoon cumin seeds

1 teaspoon ground coriander

1 green chilli, de-seeded and chopped finely (optional)

300 ml (10 fl oz) chicken stock

100 g (3½ oz) baby spinach, washed

300 g (10½ oz) low fat natural yogurt

a bunch of fresh coriander, chopped

salt and freshly ground black pepper

4 lemon wedges, to serve

**1** Heat a large, lidded, non stick frying pan and spray with the cooking spray. Stir-fry the chicken for 4 minutes or so until golden on the edges and white all over.

**2** Add the potatoes, onion, garlic, ginger, spices and chilli, if using, and fry for a further 4 minutes until they turn golden.

**3** Add the stock, bring to the boil and cover. Simmer gently for 15 minutes until the chicken is tender, the potatoes are cooked through and the sauce has thickened.

**4** Stir in the spinach and check the seasoning. Allow to cool a little and then stir in the yogurt and scatter with the coriander. Serve with the lemon wedges.

# Chicken chunga

Serves 4

**330 calories** per serving

Takes 35 minutes to prepare,
45 minutes to cook

calorie controlled cooking
spray

**4 x 175 g (6 oz) skinless
boneless chicken breasts**

**2.5 cm (1 inch) fresh root
ginger, chopped finely**

**1 large onion, chopped**

**1 small red chilli, de-seeded
and chopped finely**

**2 carrots, peeled and sliced**

**100 g (3½ oz) button
mushrooms**

**1 red pepper, de-seeded and
chopped**

**1 celery stick, chopped**

**1 tablespoon plain white flour**

**150 ml (5 fl oz) red or white
wine**

**300 ml (10 fl oz) chicken stock**

**400 g can black eyed beans,
drained and rinsed**

*'Chunga' is a Caribbean word for hotpot, into which
virtually anything can be thrown, so think of this recipe
as a rough guide only, and use whatever vegetables you
like. Serve with 60 g (2 oz) dried basmati rice per person,
cooked according to the packet instructions.*

**1** Preheat the oven to Gas Mark 4/180°C/fan oven 160°C. Heat
a lidded flame and ovenproof casserole dish on the hob and
spray with the cooking spray. Add the chicken and ginger, fry
for 5 minutes until browned all over and then remove from the
dish and set aside.

**2** Spray the casserole dish with the cooking spray again and
fry the onion for 5 minutes until the onion has softened. Add
the chilli and then the other vegetables and stir-fry for a few
minutes more. Remove from the dish and set aside.

**3** Sprinkle the flour into the casserole dish, mix into any juices
in the bottom and then add the wine and stir until smooth and
thick. Add the stock, bring to the boil and simmer for 5 minutes,
stirring.

**4** Return the chicken, ginger, vegetables and chilli to the
casserole dish, cover and bake in the oven for 45 minutes. Add
the beans to the casserole dish 10 minutes before the end of
the cooking time.

# Kofta in red curry sauce

**Serves 2**

**305 calories** per serving

Takes 20 minutes to prepare + chilling, 20 minutes to cook

❄ (meatballs and sauce separately if uncooked)

**200 g (7 oz) lean minced beef**

**1 garlic clove, chopped**

**1 tablespoon chopped fresh root ginger**

**½ teaspoon ground cumin**

**1 tablespoon chopped fresh coriander, plus extra to garnish**

**1 small egg, beaten lightly**

**2 small onions, chopped finely**

**salt and freshly ground black pepper**

For the sauce

**calorie controlled cooking spray**

**2 garlic cloves, chopped finely**

**1 tablespoon tandoori curry powder**

**1 teaspoon ground coriander**

**1 teaspoon ground cumin**

**400 g can chopped tomatoes**

**4 tablespoons 0% fat Greek yogurt**

*Meatballs in a creamy sauce are perfect for a special meal.*

**1** Put the mince, garlic, ginger, cumin, coriander and egg in a food processor with half the onions. Season and blend to a coarse paste. Using wet hands, shape the mixture into walnut size balls, put them on a plate and chill, covered, for about 30 minutes.

**2** To make the sauce, spray a lidded non stick frying pan with the cooking spray and fry the remaining onion for 7 minutes, adding a little water if necessary to prevent it from sticking. Add the garlic and spices and cook for 30 seconds.

**3** Pour in the tomatoes and 5 tablespoons of water. Bring to the boil and then reduce the heat to simmering point. Arrange the meatballs in the pan, cover and simmer for 15–20 minutes, turning occasionally and adding a little water if the sauce looks too dry, until the balls are cooked through.

**4** When the meatballs are cooked, remove them from the pan using a slotted spoon and arrange on two plates. Stir the yogurt into the pan and season. Heat through gently and spoon the sauce over the meatballs. Garnish with the extra coriander.

# Chermoula curried pork

Serves 6
**179 calories** per serving
Takes 25 minutes
❄

6 x 110 g (4 oz) lean pork loin steaks, trimmed of visible fat
1 tablespoon medium curry powder
calorie controlled cooking spray
300 ml (10 fl oz) hot chicken stock
150 g (5½ oz) low fat soft cheese
1 teaspoon ground cumin
2 teaspoons paprika
2 garlic cloves, crushed
30 g (1¼ oz) jalapeño peppers from a jar, drained and chopped finely
2 tablespoons chopped fresh coriander
2 limes, cut into wedges, to serve

*Chermoula is a spicy herb sauce that will infuse any dish with lovely piquant flavours. Serve with 150 g (5½ oz) cooked bulgur wheat per person and cooked spinach.*

**1** Coat the pork steaks all over with the curry powder. Heat a wide, deep, non stick frying pan and spray the pork steaks with the cooking spray. Cook the steaks for 10 minutes, turning until brown all over. Remove, cover with foil and set aside.

**2** Add a splash of the stock to the hot frying pan to deglaze it and then stir in the soft cheese, cumin, paprika, garlic and jalapeño peppers.

**3** Gradually stir in the remaining stock. Bring to the boil and simmer for 2 minutes. Return the pork steaks to the pan and then simmer for 1 minute. Scatter over the coriander and serve with the lime wedges.

# Vegetable couscous with harissa

Serves 4
**560 calories** per serving
Takes 20 minutes to prepare, 30 minutes to cook ♥

*Don't be put off by the long list of ingredients, this is well worth the effort.*

450 g (1 lb) dried couscous
a kettleful of boiling water
calorie controlled cooking spray
2 onions, quartered
225 g (8 oz) pumpkin, peeled, de-seeded and diced
225 g (8 oz) carrots, peeled and sliced
2 garlic cloves, crushed
a pinch of saffron strands
2 cinnamon sticks
2 tablespoons coriander seeds, crushed
1 teaspoon paprika
1 red chilli
225 g (8 oz) tomatoes, diced
225 g (8 oz) courgettes, sliced

50 g (1¾ oz) raisins
175 g (6 oz) shelled fresh or frozen broad beans
450 ml (16 fl oz) vegetable stock
salt and freshly ground black pepper
a bunch of fresh coriander, chopped roughly, to garnish

For the harissa
2 tablespoons tomato purée
1 garlic clove, crushed
1 teaspoon cayenne pepper
1 teaspoon ground coriander
1 teaspoon ground cumin
4 fresh mint sprigs, chopped finely

**1** Put the couscous in a bowl and pour over enough boiling water to cover it plus 2.5 cm (1 inch). Cover the bowl with a plate or cling film and set aside to steam.

**2** Spray a large non stick pan with the cooking spray and sauté the onions for 4 minutes, adding a little water if necessary to prevent them from sticking. Add the pumpkin, carrots and garlic and cook for another 3 minutes. Add the saffron, cinnamon, coriander seeds, paprika and whole chilli. Lower the heat, cover and cook for 5 minutes.

*continues overleaf* ▶

**3** Add the tomatoes and courgettes to the pan with the raisins, broad beans and stock. Season and then cook, uncovered, for 20 minutes. Stir frequently until the vegetables are tender and the stock has been reduced and thickened.

**4** Make the harissa by mixing together all the ingredients and then add 4 tablespoons of the liquid from the stew.

**5** Remove the plate or cling film from the couscous and fluff up with a fork. Put on serving plates. Remove the cinnamon sticks from the stew and then spoon the stew over the couscous. Serve with the harissa and sprinkled with the coriander.

**Tip...** You can also buy ready-made harissa rather than making your own.

# Peppered trout with watercress sauce

Serves 2
**290 calories** per serving
Takes 25 minutes
❄

4 x 75 g (2¾ oz) skinless trout fillets
4 teaspoons lemon juice
freshly ground mixed pepper

For the sauce
150 g (5½ oz) watercress
100 ml (3½ fl oz) vegetable stock
1 teaspoon horseradish sauce
3 tablespoons half fat crème fraîche
1 tablespoon cornflour
2 tablespoons skimmed milk

*The combination of mixed pepper, watercress and horseradish makes this quite hot.*

**1** Line a baking tray with non stick baking parchment. Rinse the trout fillets and pat them dry with kitchen towel. Place them on the baking tray and season well with mixed pepper. Preheat the grill to medium.

**2** Drizzle the lemon juice over the fish and grill the fish for 5–6 minutes until the fillets are cooked through.

**3** Meanwhile, place the watercress in a pan with the stock. Simmer for 2 minutes until the watercress wilts. Transfer it to a food processor or use a hand blender and whizz until smooth. Return the sauce to a clean pan and stir in the horseradish sauce and crème fraîche.

**4** Mix the cornflour with the milk to make a thin paste and stir this into the pan. Cook, stirring, until the sauce thickens a little.

**5** Transfer two cooked trout fillets per person to warmed serving plates and drizzle over the watercress sauce.

**Tip...** Hand blenders are very good and inexpensive, perfect for blending sauces and soups – what's more they are so easy to wash too.

# Spicy pasta and cockles

Serves 4
**405 calories** per serving
Takes 25 minutes

**350 g (12 oz) dried spaghetti
or tagliatelle**
**calorie controlled cooking
spray**
**2 garlic cloves, crushed**
**4 courgettes, diced finely**
**1 small red chilli, de-seeded
and chopped finely**
**2 x 205 g jars cockles, drained
and rinsed**
**2 tablespoons soy sauce**
**juice of a lime**
**a small bunch of fresh
coriander or parsley,
chopped, to garnish
(optional)**

*A scrumptious, quick and spicy recipe, good for lunch or
dinner.*

**1** Bring a pan of water to the boil, add the pasta and cook
according to the packet instructions, until just tender.

**2** Meanwhile, heat a large non stick frying pan and spray with
the cooking spray. Fry the garlic for 1 minute and then add the
courgettes and stir-fry for 4 minutes until golden brown around
the edges.

**3** Add the chilli, cockles and soy sauce and stir-fry for a further
2 minutes. Add the lime juice and take off the heat.

**4** Drain the pasta, add the cockles and sauce to the pan and
toss together. Serve immediately, sprinkled with the coriander
or parsley, if using.

# Thai grilled chicken

Serves 4

**370 calories** per serving

Takes 10 minutes to prepare +
marinating, 15–20 minutes
to cook

**1 large garlic clove, crushed**

**2 teaspoons ready-prepared
lemongrass from a jar**

**2 teaspoons finely grated
fresh root ginger**

**1 tablespoon Thai red curry
paste**

**finely grated zest and juice of
2 limes**

**2 tablespoons chopped fresh
coriander**

**4 x 150 g (5½ oz) skinless
boneless chicken breasts**

**225 g (8 oz) dried jasmine or
basmati rice**

**salt and freshly ground black
pepper**

To garnish

**4 lime slices**

**a few fresh coriander sprigs**

*This is very quick and easy but full of the flavours of
Thailand. Serve with a large green salad.*

**1** In a glass or plastic bowl, mix together the garlic,
lemongrass, ginger, curry paste, lime zest, lime juice and
chopped coriander. Season, add the chicken breasts, turn to
coat in the mixture and then cover and refrigerate for at least
30 minutes.

**2** Preheat the grill to medium high. Put the chicken breasts on
the grill rack and cook for about 15–20 minutes, turning once
and basting with the marinade from time to time.

**3** Meanwhile, bring a pan of water to the boil, add the rice
and cook for about 12 minutes, or according to the packet
instructions, until tender. Drain well.

**4** Check that the chicken breasts are thoroughly cooked by
piercing the thickest part with a sharp knife. The juices should
run clear. If not, cook for a little longer. Serve the chicken and
rice garnished with lime slices and coriander sprigs.

**Tip... You can buy ready-prepared lemongrass, ginger and
garlic in handy small jars from most large supermarkets.
Keep refrigerated once opened.**

# Baked coriander cod

Serves 4
**143 calories** per serving
Takes 20 minutes

**2 tablespoons finely chopped fresh coriander**

**1 teaspoon grated fresh root ginger**

**1 garlic clove, crushed**

**10 freeze dried curry leaves, crushed**

**25 g (1 oz) creamed coconut, grated**

**4 x 125 g (4½ oz) skinless cod loin fillets**

**salt and freshly ground black pepper**

*Serve with 100 g (3½ oz) boiled potato chunks per person, sautéed in calorie controlled cooking spray and seasoned with a little cayenne pepper, as well as steamed tenderstem broccoli and carrots.*

**1** Preheat the oven to Gas Mark 5/190°C/fan oven 170°C and put a baking tray or ovenproof dish in the oven to heat.

**2** In a bowl, mix together the coriander, ginger, garlic, curry leaves and coconut and season.

**3** Place the cod loin fillets on a board and press a little of the coriander mixture on to each fillet. Remove the baking tray or ovenproof dish from the oven, transfer the cod to the tray or dish and bake in the oven for 10 minutes until cooked. Serve immediately.

# Chilli polenta wedges

Serves 4
**239 calories** per serving
Takes 20 minutes

850 ml (1½ pints) hot vegetable stock

a generous pinch of saffron strands

200 g (7 oz) dried easy cook polenta

3 cardamom pods, seeds removed and crushed

198 g can sweetcorn, drained

2 tablespoons roughly chopped fresh coriander

3 spring onions, sliced finely

calorie controlled cooking spray

300 g (10½ oz) mixed mushrooms, sliced

1 red chilli, de-seeded and chopped finely

4 tablespoons low fat natural yogurt

salt and freshly ground black pepper

*Serve with half an avocado, a tomato and a mixed salad tossed with 1 tablespoon of fat free salad dressing per person.*

**1** Put the vegetable stock and saffron into a large saucepan and bring to the boil. Quickly add the polenta, stirring until it forms a smooth mixture. Gently bubble for 1 minute, stirring, and then stir in the cardamom seeds, sweetcorn, coriander, spring onions and seasoning. Cook for 2–3 minutes and then pour into a 20 cm (8 inch) loose-bottomed, round cake tin and level the top. Cover with foil and set aside for 10 minutes.

**2** Meanwhile, heat a lidded non stick frying pan and spray with the cooking spray. Cook the mushrooms and chilli, covered, on a low heat for 5–8 minutes, until soft.

**3** Cut the polenta into four wedges and top each serving with the mushrooms and a tablespoon of yogurt.

**Variation...** For a non vegetarian option, try adding 100 g (3½ oz) diced cooked chicken with the mushrooms.

# Spicy turkey marrow

Serves 4

**209 calories** per serving

Takes 25 minutes to prepare,
35–40 minutes to cook

1 marrow, halved lengthways
  and de-seeded
2 teaspoons vegetable oil
1 onion, chopped
1 carrot, peeled and grated
1 red pepper, de-seeded and
  chopped
2 garlic cloves, crushed
1 tablespoon mild curry
  powder or mixed spice
275 g (9½ oz) minced turkey
2 tablespoons chopped fresh
  herbs or 1 tablespoon dried
  mixed herbs
1 tablespoon soy sauce
150 ml (5 fl oz) chicken stock
2 tablespoons half fat crème
  fraîche
salt and freshly ground black
  pepper

*This makes a great centrepiece for a meal with friends.*

**1** Preheat the oven to Gas Mark 6/200°C/fan oven 180°F.
Place the marrow in a large baking dish or roasting tin, cut
sides facing up.

**2** Heat the oil in a large non stick pan, add the onion and sauté
gently for 2–3 minutes. Add the carrot, red pepper and garlic and
cook gently for another 3–4 minutes until softened. Stir in the
curry powder or mixed spice and cook for 1 minute more.

**3** Stir the mince into the vegetables and then add the herbs
and soy sauce. Cook for 2–3 minutes over a medium-high heat
and then add the stock. Heat until boiling, reduce the heat and
simmer for about 10 minutes, uncovered, until the stock has
been reduced by half. Season to taste.

**4** Remove from the heat and stir in the crème fraîche. Spoon the
mixture into the hollowed out marrow. Add about 150 ml (5 fl oz)
of cold water to the baking dish or tin around the marrow, cover
the dish with foil and bake for 35–40 minutes, until the marrow
is tender.

# Spiced chicken parcels

Serves 4
**265 calories** per serving
Takes 10 minutes to prepare,
40 minutes to cook

*The chicken steams in these little packages, making it really juicy. Add 150 g (5½ oz) diced potatoes per person, sautéed in calorie controlled cooking spray until golden and crispy.*

30 g (1¼ oz) low fat spread
2 large carrots, peeled and cut into batons
4 x 165 g (5¾ oz) skinless boneless chicken breasts
2 tablespoons clear honey
2 garlic cloves, sliced
4 star anise
2 cinnamon sticks, broken in half
8 cardamon pods, split
150 ml (5 fl oz) dry white wine

**1** Preheat the oven to Gas Mark 4/180°C/fan oven 160°C. Arrange four pieces of foil, each measuring 30 x 30 cm (12 x 12 inches), on a clean surface. Divide the low fat spread and carrot sticks between the foil squares, putting them in the centre of each square, and top each with a chicken breast.

**2** Drizzle each chicken breast with ½ tablespoon of honey and then scatter over half a garlic clove, 1 star anise, half a cinnamon stick and two cardamon pods. Fold up the sides of each foil square to make a parcel, leaving an opening in the top. Pour a quarter of the wine into each parcel and then seal completely.

**3** Put the parcels on a baking tray and bake in the oven for 40 minutes until cooked. To serve, open the parcels, discard the spices and serve each chicken breast with the carrots and the juices drizzled over.

# Red lentil and aubergine curry

Serves 4
**210 calories** per serving
Takes 45 minutes

❄

calorie controlled cooking
spray
1 onion, chopped
2 garlic cloves, crushed
2 tablespoons medium curry
powder
1 aubergine, diced
175 g (6 oz) dried red lentils
600 ml (20 fl oz) vegetable
stock
100 ml (3½ fl oz) reduced fat
coconut milk
2 tablespoons chopped fresh
coriander

*The lentils, aubergine and coconut combine beautifully to
make a lovely rich sauce.*

**1** Spray a non stick frying pan with the cooking spray and
gently cook the onion and garlic until softened, but not
browned. Stir in the curry powder and cook for 1 minute.

**2** Add the aubergine, lentils and stock to the pan. Bring to the
boil and simmer, uncovered, for 30 minutes, stirring regularly to
prevent the lentils from sticking.

**3** After 30 minutes the lentils should be tender and mushy
– if not raise the heat and boil vigorously for 5 minutes. Add
the coconut milk and coriander and mix well. Heat through
and serve.

**Variation...** If you wish, leave out the coconut milk and stir
in 2 tablespoons of tomato purée instead.

# Chilli crusted lamb cutlets

**Serves 4**
**505 calories** per serving
Takes 25 minutes

3 large red chillies, de-seeded
  and chopped
2 spring onions, chopped
3 tablespoons lemon juice
2 tablespoons chopped fresh
  coriander
8 lamb cutlets
salt and freshly ground black
  pepper

For the raita
¼ cucumber, grated
200 g (7 fl oz) low fat natural
  yogurt
1 tablespoon chopped fresh
  mint

*Serve these simple spicy cutlets with peas or steamed green vegetables of your choice.*

**1** Preheat the grill to medium high. Whizz the chillies, spring onions, lemon juice and coriander in a food processor until roughly chopped.

**2** Spread the mixture over both sides of the cutlets and season well. Place the cutlets on a non stick baking tray and cook under the grill for 3–4 minutes on each side or until cooked to your liking.

**3** Meanwhile, mix the raita ingredients together. Serve with the cutlets.

# Index

## Other titles in the Weight Watchers Mini Series

ISBN 978-0-85720-932-0

ISBN 978-0-85720-935-1

ISBN 978-0-85720-934-4

ISBN 978-0-85720-938-2

ISBN 978-0-85720-931-3

ISBN 978-0-85720-937-5

ISBN 978-0-85720-936-8

ISBN 978-0-85720-933-7

ISBN 978-1-47111-084-9

ISBN 978-1-47111-089-4

ISBN 978-1-47111-091-7

ISBN 978-1-47111-087-0

ISBN 978-1-47111-090-0

ISBN 978-1-47111-085-6

ISBN 978-1-47111-088-7

ISBN 978-1-47111-086-3

For more details please visit www.simonandschuster.co.uk